marie claire

spicy

Published by Murdoch Books Pty Limited.
www.murdochbooks.com.au

Murdoch Books Australia
Pier 8/9, 23 Hickson Rd
Millers Point NSW 2000
Phone: +61 (0)2 8220 2000
Fax: +61 (0)2 8220 2558

Murdoch Books UK Limited
Erico House, 6th Floor North
93–99 Upper Richmond Road
Putney, London SW15 2TG
Phone: +44 (0)20 8785 5995
Fax: +44 (0)20 8785 5985

Author and Stylist: Michele Cranston
Photographer: Petrina Tinslay
Design manager: Vivien Valk
Concept: Lauren Camilleri
Designer: Jacqueline Richards
Editor: Gordana Trifunovic
Food preparation: Ross Dobson and Jo Glynn
Production: Monika Paratore

Chief executive: Juliet Rogers
Publisher: Kay Scarlett

National Library of Australia Cataloguing-in-Publication Data
Cranston, Michele. Marie Claire spicy. Includes index.
ISBN 1 74045 749 8 / 978 1 74045 749 1
1. Cookery. 2. Spices I. Title. II. Title: Spicy. III. Title: Marie Claire (North Sydney, N.S.W.).
641.6383

Printed by 1010 Printing International Ltd. Printed in China. First printed 2006.

Important: Those who might be at risk from the effects of salmonella poisoning (the elderly, pregnant women, young children and those suffering from immune deficiency diseases) should consult their doctor with any concerns about eating raw eggs.

Conversion guide: You may find cooking times vary depending on the oven you are using. For fan-forced ovens, as a general rule, set the oven temperature to 20°C (35°F) lower than indicated in the recipe. We have used 20 ml (4 teaspoon) tablespoon measures. If you are using a 15 ml (3 teaspoon) tablespoon, for most recipes the difference will not be noticeable. However, for recipes using baking powder, gelatine, bicarbonate of soda (baking soda) or small amounts of flour and cornflour, add an extra teaspoon for each tablespoon specified.

marie claire
spicy

michele cranston
photography by petrina tinslay

MURDOCH BOOKS

contents

introduction   6

01   starters and sides   16

02   light meals   94

03   mains   150

04   sweets   224

05   drinks   312

06   basics   350

glossary   388

index   394

Welcome to *marie claire spicy,* a selection of our favourite recipes that are warm and inviting, richly flavoured, sweetly spiced or just simple food with a bit of a twist. A thick and hearty book with lots of yummy ideas that we hope will inspire you, everything from easy dips and spiced nuts through to peppered beef, richly flavoured curries and exotic desserts.

I've had a lot of fun revisiting old favourites and I hope that you have as much fun cooking and eating from our selection.

michele cranston

ingredient note   # figs

A perfect fig is a wonderful thing to behold — and to sink
your teeth into. I first fell in love with figs when
backpacking through Greece. Up and about early in the morning
I stumbled upon a market square. One of the stalls had big
vats of creamy yoghurt. The yoghurt was served in a cup with
a swirl of wild honey and the stall next door sold fresh
figs, straight from the tree, warmed by the early morning
sun. I don't think I've had a better breakfast!

However, figs are one of those rare fruits which do have a
distinct season and they are only available on the shop
shelves for a short time. So when they do finally appear,
don't just limit their use to the odd sumptuous breakfast,
they can and should be enjoyed at any time of the day. Served
with goat's cheese, rocket (arugula) leaves and a sweet
balsamic dressing they become an indulgent lunch. Wrapped
around prosciutto they make a wonderful start to an evening
meal and with a pile of muscatels they make the perfect
accompaniment to a selection of soft cheeses.

Figs love spices, nuts and cream so there really is no excuse
not to use them for a tempting selection of desserts. They
can be baked into a tart of sugary sweetness or freshly
sliced over small tartlets filled with sweet mascarpone. Bake
them whole with the addition of soft brown sugar and Marsala,
arrange fresh slices over meringue or simply cut in half,
sprinkle with sugar and grill (broil). That's the great thing
about figs — already so perfect, they need very little work
to turn them into a celebratory ending to any meal.

ingredient note

rhubarb

I have to admit to a love of rhubarb which goes back to my childhood. My grandfather had wonderful vegetable garden and one section was devoted to rhubarb. As a young child I would gaze at the exuberant red stalks that stood out from the green mass of fresh herbs, spinach leaves and carrot tops. As a result, my grandfather always seemed to have a bowl of stewed rhubarb in the refrigerator, which would be spooned over ice cream, custard and even the odd bowl of breakfast cereal.

Rhubarb is actually a vegetable and while it can be used in stews with meat it really comes into its own when cooked with just enough sugar to cut its sharpness. Always look for stalks that are a rich red and which show no signs of softening. Trim the leaves and cut the rhubarb into small pieces before cooking over a low heat with some sugar or with the addition of orange juice, vanilla, star anise or fresh ginger.

Rhubarb is available all year round, making it an ideal addition to the dessert repertoire in those cooler months when the fruit selection can seem a little dismal. It's wonderful added to apple and pear for a winter crumble, stewed and spooned over mini pavlovas or served alongside crème brûlées to cut their richness. For a lighter touch simply bake and serve with creamy custard and amaretti biscuits or fold a purée of rhubarb through whipped cream for a simple tangy dessert.

ingredient note

eggplant

There really is something quite beautiful about an eggplant (aubergine). I always think they look as if they've been sculpted into shape and then heavily burnished to that wonderful purple-black colour. I have to admit that I do often buy them merely as beautiful objects to put in my kitchen. Fortunately I also love to eat them, so there's no waste!

Eggplants grilled over a barbecue or gas flame take on a wonderful smoky flavour which makes for a perfect dip when mixed with a bit of lemon juice, tahini and a light scatter of parsley leaves. Barbecued slices can be tossed with parsley, coriander (cilantro) or basil and added to tomato and pine nuts for a simple vegetable side dish. Fried in small bite-sized chunks it becomes a meaty addition to vegetable stews and curries or a hearty addition to that famous eggplant dish, moussaka. Thinly sliced and deep fried they make a great addition to any salad or can be used crisp for dipping. While usually associated with European and Middle Eastern cooking, the eggplant also works well with the Asian flavours of soy, ginger and chilli as well as being an important ingredient in many Thai curries.

There seems to be some debate as to whether eggplants need to be salted. This time-consuming process shouldn't be necessary with small or very fresh eggplant. The salting is merely to draw out any bitterness, which can sometimes occur in older or larger eggplants. However salting does help if you need to fry the eggplant as the process prevents the pieces from soaking up too much oil.

ingredient note   saffron

There's something evocative about spices. Whenever I use them
I try to remember that there is a wonderful history of
ancient trade routes and people travelling long distances to
discover new cuisines with exotic tastes and aromas. If ever
a spice lived up to such heady notions then saffron is the
one. Each golden strand is hand picked from the purple crocus
flower. It is then dried and sold as, not surprisingly, a
very expensive spice. But don't let the price stop you from
buying a small amount, especially if it comes from Spain
which reputedly harvests the best in the world. You only need
a small amount when you're cooking and it really does infuse
any meal with a wonderful taste and a golden hue.

As a flavour saffron is ideally suited to seafood dishes and
makes an appearance in such classics as bouillabaisse and
paella. While perfectly suited to seafood, it can also be
used with vegetables and fruit. For a golden dessert, add a
tiny amount to the poaching liquid for pears or toss a little
saffron-tinged water in with leeks that have been basted in
lots of butter, salt, pepper and a little chicken stock.

To get the most out of your saffron I find it is best to
first heat it over a low flame in the base of a saucepan and
to then pour over a little water, allowing the intense
flavour and yellow colour to be transferred to the liquid. It
is then quite easy to add it to any dishes whether they be
baked, stewed or simmered.

beetroot dip bread sticks tabouleh eggplant pinwheels quail eggs with za'atar mix eggplant dip spiced nut blend baby eggplant with grilled miso spiced potato crisps spicy nut biscuits eggplant rounds with sweet harissa and mint hummus watermelon squares welsh rarebit chilli beef on endive leaves lime and cashew blue-eye cod rolls gravlax with dill dressing on pumpernickel and pepper tofu spiced pan

01 starters and sides

bread taramasalata sweet potato crisps with baba ghanoush roast vegetables with rouille spiced red cabbage fennel salad burghul salad roast beetroot salad papaya and coconut sambal warm banana chilli salad puy lentil and spinach salad fattoush spiced

beetroot dip

serves 6-8

4 large beetroot (beets)
250 g (9 oz/1 cup) Greek-style yoghurt
1 teaspoon pomegranate molasses
10 mint leaves, finely chopped
10 walnuts, finely chopped
toasted pitta bread, to serve

Preheat the oven to 200°C (400°F/ Gas 6). Place the beetroot in a roasting dish with 250 ml (9 fl oz/ 1 cup) of water. Cover with foil and roast for 1 hour, or until cooked. Rub the skin off the beetroot.

Place the beetroot in a food processor or blender and blend to a smooth paste. Put in a bowl and stir in the yoghurt and molasses. Season to taste with sea salt and freshly ground black pepper. Garnish with the mint and walnuts and serve with toasted pitta bread.

bread sticks

2 teaspoons dry yeast
1/2 teaspoon sugar
310 g (11 oz/2 1/2 cups) plain
   (all-purpose) flour
2 tablespoons black sesame seeds
1 tablespoon freshly ground cumin
   seeds
2 tablespoons chopped thyme
1 egg
1 tablespoon olive oil

Mix the yeast, 250 ml (9 fl oz/1 cup) of warm water and the sugar in a bowl. Leave to sit for 10 minutes. Put the flour, sesame seeds, cumin, thyme and 1/2 teaspoon of salt in a bowl and make a well in the centre. Pour in the yeast mixture and mix to form a soft dough. Gather into a ball, turn out onto a floured surface and knead for 10 minutes. Place in an oiled bowl and cover with plastic wrap. Leave for 3 hours in a warm place. When doubled in size, punch down and turn out onto a floured surface, then knead for 2 minutes. Roll the dough out to a thickness of 5 mm (1/4 in). Cut into strips approximately 25 x 1 cm (10 x 1/2 in). Roll and place onto baking trays lined with baking paper. Cover and allow to rise for 30 minutes.

Preheat the oven to 180°C (350°F/ Gas 4). In a bowl, beat the egg with 3 tablespoons of water. Brush the dough with the egg wash. Bake for 15 minutes, or until golden. Remove from the oven, brush with olive oil and sprinkle with sea salt. Return to the oven for a further 4–5 minutes, or until golden. Allow to cool on a wire rack.

tabouleh

70 g (2¹/₂ oz/heaped ¹/₃ cup) burghul
  (bulgur)
3 ripe tomatoes, finely chopped
150 g (5¹/₂ oz) flat-leaf (Italian) parsley
2 spring onions (scallions), finely
  chopped
1 small handful mint, finely chopped
4 tablespoons olive oil
3 tablespoons lemon juice

Soak the burghul in cold water for 10 minutes, then drain and squeeze to remove any excess water. Put the burghul in a large bowl and add the tomatoes. Season with sea salt and freshly ground black pepper. Finely chop the parsley, gathering the leafy ends together and discarding the stems. Add to the salad with the onions and mint. Combine the olive oil and lemon juice and pour over the salad. Toss together and serve.

eggplant pinwheels   makes 20

2 red capsicums (peppers), trimmed
and seeds removed
400 g (14 oz) zucchini (courgettes)
50 large basil leaves
1 tablespoon balsamic vinegar
3 tablespoons olive oil
1 large eggplant (aubergine), thinly
sliced lengthways

Grill (broil) or roast the capsicums and set aside to cool. With a vegetable peeler, slice the zucchini into long ribbons. Blanch in boiling water for a few seconds and refresh in cold water. Repeat with the basil leaves. Peel the cooked capsicums and slice the flesh in half. Toss with the vinegar.

Heat the oil in a large frying pan over medium heat and cook the eggplant slices until soft. Drain on paper towels. Lay a piece of plastic wrap or baking paper on the work surface and arrange a single line of overlapping eggplant slices. Cover with a layer of zucchini, then a layer of capsicum and finally a layer of basil leaves. Roll up firmly to form a thin log. Repeat with the remaining ingredients. Refrigerate until ready to use. Slice and serve.

quail eggs with za'atar mix

2 tablespoons sesame seeds, lightly
   toasted
1 tablespoon thyme leaves
1 tablespoon ground sumac
1/2 teaspoon ground cumin
24 quail eggs, boiled and shelled

Mix together the sesame seeds and
spices along with 1 teaspoon of sea
salt. Serve in a bowl accompanied by
the quail eggs.

eggplant dip

2 tablespoons oil
1 garlic bulb
1 large eggplant (aubergine)
4 tablespoons tahini
2 tablespoons lemon juice
2 tablespoons finely chopped flat-leaf
  (Italian) parsley
sprinkle of cayenne pepper, to garnish
slices of crusty bread, to serve

Preheat the oven to 200°C (400°F/ Gas 6). Put the oil in a small roasting dish. Cut the garlic bulb across the middle so that the cloves are cut in half. Put each half garlic bulb cut side down in the oiled dish and add the eggplant. Bake for 20 minutes, or until the garlic halves are golden brown and the eggplant is soft. Remove from the oven and allow to cool. With the tip of a small sharp knife, separate the garlic cloves from the bulb and put them in a blender or food processor. Cut the eggplant in half, scoop out the soft flesh and add it to the garlic. Blend to a purée. Transfer to a bowl and fold through the tahini and lemon juice. Season with sea salt. Just before serving, fold through the parsley and garnish with a sprinkle of cayenne pepper. Serve with crusty bread.

spiced nut blend

makes 350 g (12 oz)

1 teaspoon cumin seeds
1 teaspoon coriander seeds
1 teaspoon mustard seeds
1/4 teaspoon fennel seeds
1/2 cinnamon stick
1/2 teaspoon black peppercorns
1 teaspoon ground turmeric
2 tablespoons soft brown sugar
350 g (12 oz) mixed nuts, including
   pecans, cashew nuts, peanuts and
   macadamia nuts
2 teaspoons sea salt
2 tablespoons olive oil

Preheat the oven to 160°C (315°F/ Gas 2–3). Place all the spices in a spice grinder or blender and grind to a fine powder. Transfer the mixture to a large bowl and mix through the brown sugar, nuts and the sea salt. Add the olive oil, mix well and place on a baking tray. Bake for 10–15 minutes, or until the nuts have coloured a little. Allow to cool. Store in an airtight container until ready to serve.

baby eggplant
with grilled miso

makes 20

80 g (2³/4 oz) white miso paste
1 tablespoon sugar
1 tablespoon mirin
1 egg yolk
2 teaspoons fresh ginger juice
10 baby eggplants (aubergines)
200 ml (7 fl oz) vegetable oil
1 tablespoon sesame seeds

Put the miso, sugar and mirin in a large bowl, add the egg yolk and lightly whisk. Place the bowl over a saucepan of boiling water, whisking continuously while slowly adding 4 tablespoons of cold water. Keep whisking until the mixture is thick. Stir through the ginger juice.

Preheat the oven to 190°C (375°F/Gas 5). Slice each of the eggplants in half lengthways and trim the skin side so that the halves will sit flat. Heat the oil in a deep frying pan over medium heat and cook the eggplants on both sides until they are golden and slightly soft. Remove and drain on paper towels. Place the eggplants on a baking tray and spread with a little of the miso paste. Sprinkle with sesame seeds and bake for 5 minutes.

spiced potato crisps

makes 30

1 teaspoon sesame seeds
1/2 teaspoon ground cumin
1/2 teaspoon ground coriander
1/2 teaspoon ground paprika
2 large roasting potatoes, peeled
20 g (3/4 oz) unsalted butter, melted

Preheat the oven to 170°C (325°F/ Gas 3). Combine the sesame seeds, spices and herbs in a small bowl. Slice the potatoes very thinly and place half the slices on a baking tray lined with baking paper. Top each slice of potato with another slice, preferably of a similar size, and press together. (The starch in the potatoes will stick them together.) Brush with butter and sprinkle with the spice mix.

Bake for 45 minutes, or until the potatoes are crisp and golden brown. Drain on paper towels and serve.

spicy nut biscuits   makes 55

1 tablespoon grated fresh ginger
1 green chilli, seeded and finely
   chopped
200 g (7 oz/1 1/3 cups) cashew nuts
100 g (3 1/2 oz/2/3 cup) pistachio nuts
200 g (7 oz) rice flour
1 1/2 teaspoons ground cumin
2 tablespoons roughly chopped
   coriander (cilantro) leaves
1 tablespoon black sesame seeds
20 g (3/4 oz) butter
2 eggs, beaten
150 ml (5 fl oz) vegetable oil

Put the ginger, chilli, cashew nuts, pistachios, rice flour, cumin, coriander, sesame seeds, butter and 2 teaspoons of salt in a food processor. Pulse a few times to grind the nuts, then transfer to a large bowl. Add the eggs and 3 tablespoons of water. Stir until the mixture combines and is sticky.

Take a heaped teaspoon of the mixture, roll into a ball and flatten slightly. Heat the oil in a deep frying pan over low heat. Take a few of the flattened balls and place into the oil. Cook for 5 minutes, turning once, until golden brown. Drain on paper towels. Repeat with the remaining mixture.

eggplant rounds with sweet harissa and mint

makes 24

4 baby or Japanese eggplants
 (aubergines)
150 ml (5 fl oz) vegetable oil
2 red capsicums (peppers), roasted,
 skins removed
2 teaspoons roasted ground cumin
2 teaspoons roasted ground coriander
2 small red chillies, seeded and finely
 chopped
1/2 teaspoon ground paprika
1 large handful roughly chopped
 flat-leaf (Italian) parsley
2 large handfuls roughly chopped
 coriander (cilantro) leaves
2 garlic cloves
3 tablespoons olive oil
6 mint leaves
1/2 teaspoon soft brown sugar
24 mint leaves, extra, to serve

Trim the ends off the eggplants and cut them into 2 cm (3/4 in) discs. Place in a colander over a bowl and lightly salt. Allow to sit for 30 minutes before rinsing and squeezing dry. Heat the oil in a deep frying pan over moderate heat and cook the eggplant rounds in batches until golden, turning once. Drain on paper towels.

Make the harissa by placing the roasted capsicum, cumin, coriander, chilli, paprika, parsley, fresh coriander, garlic, olive oil, mint leaves, sugar and 1 teaspoon of salt in a blender and blending to form a smooth paste. Place 1/2 teaspoon amounts of harissa onto each of the eggplant rounds, top with a fresh mint leaf and serve.

Note – This mix makes more harissa than you need, but it will keep in the refrigerator in a sealed container for 5 days. Serve with barbecued fish, chicken or roasted vegetables.

hummus

175 g (6 oz) cooked chickpeas
2 tablespoons lemon juice
3 tablespoons tahini
1 teaspoon ground cumin
1 garlic clove
pinch of cayenne pepper
2 tablespoons extra virgin olive oil

Put the chickpeas, lemon juice, tahini, cumin, garlic and cayenne pepper into a blender or food processor. Blend to a purée, adding a little water if necessary to make it smooth. Season with sea salt and freshly ground black pepper, then fold through the oil.

watermelon squares

makes 25

½ large seedless watermelon
50 g (1¾ oz) feta cheese
1 teaspoon sumac
6 black olives, seeded and finely sliced
1½ tablespoons finely chopped
  flat-leaf (Italian) parsley
1 teaspoon finely chopped thyme

Cut the watermelon flesh into 3 cm (1¼ in) cubes. Using a melon baller, remove a scoop of watermelon from the top of each cube. Set the cubes aside. Cut the feta into 1 cm (½ in) cubes and place a piece into the top of each of the watermelon cubes. Toss the sumac, sliced olives, parsley and thyme together in a small bowl, then place a small amount on top of each of the feta squares. Serve immediately.

welsh rarebit

30 g (1 oz) butter
2 tablespoons plain (all-purpose) flour
2 teaspoons wholegrain mustard
125 ml (4 fl oz/1/2 cup) Guinness or
   stout
1/2 teaspoon Worcestershire sauce
150 g (51/2 oz) mature cheddar, grated
9 slices white bread, crusts removed
   and lightly toasted

Preheat the oven to 180°C (350°F/ Gas 4). Melt the butter in a small saucepan over medium heat and stir in the flour. Add 1 teaspoon of salt, some freshly ground black pepper and the mustard, and continue to stir until the mixture begins to turn golden brown. Add the Guinness and Worcestershire sauce and whisk until the mixture is smooth and quite thick. Add three-quarters of the grated cheese and continue to whisk until the cheese has melted. Spread thickly onto the pieces of toast and sprinkle with the remaining cheese. Place in the oven for 10 minutes. Remove and slice into squares. Serve warm.

chilli beef on witlof

serves 4-6

125 ml (4 fl oz/1/2 cup) peanut oil
6 cm (21/2 in) piece fresh ginger, peeled
   and julienned
500 g (1 lb 2 oz) minced (ground) lean
   beef
3 large red chillies, seeded and finely
   chopped
2 garlic cloves, crushed
1 teaspoon sesame oil
1 teaspoon balsamic vinegar
2 teaspoons soy sauce
4 tablespoons oyster sauce
10 basil leaves, finely sliced
4 whole witlof (chicory/Belgian endive),
   washed and leaves separated

Heat the peanut oil in a frying pan over medium–high heat. Add the ginger to the oil and, once it begins to turn crisp and golden, remove and allow to drain on paper towels. Drain most of the oil from the pan, leaving just a little to coat the base, and reduce the heat to medium. Add the beef, chillies, garlic and sesame oil to the hot pan and stir-fry until the meat is cooked and beginning to brown. Add the vinegar, soy sauce and oyster sauce. Cook for a further 1–2 minutes before adding the basil leaves. Spoon the warm beef mixture into the witlof leaves and top with the fried ginger.

lime and cashew
blue-eye cod rolls   serves 4

120 g (4¹/₄ oz/1 cup) salted and roasted
  cashew nuts
1 large red chilli, seeded and roughly
  chopped
1 handful coriander (cilantro) leaves
1 teaspoon finely grated lime zest
1 tablespoon lime juice
500 g (1 lb 2 oz) blue-eye cod fillets or
  other firm whte fish fillets, divided
  into 12 portions
12 small rice paper wrappers
2 tablespoons peanut oil
2 tablespoons Chinese black vinegar or
  balsamic vinegar

Put the cashews, chilli, coriander, lime
zest and juice into a food processor or
blender and process into a paste. Put
1 tablespoon of cashew paste on the
top of each fish piece and set aside.
Dip one of the rice paper wrappers in
a bowl of water until it has softened.
Place on a dry surface and put a
piece of the fish on top. Fold the
wrapper around the fish to form a neat
parcel. Set aside and repeat with the
remaining fish.

Heat half the oil in a non-stick frying
pan over medium heat. Cook the fish
parcels for 3 minutes on each side, or
until golden brown. Add more oil when
necessary. Serve with the vinegar as a
dipping sauce.

gravlax with dill dressing on pumpernickel

makes 30

1 egg yolk
1 teaspoon wholegrain mustard
1 tablespoon lemon juice
1/2 teaspoon sugar
3 tablespoons olive oil
185 ml (6 fl oz/3/4 cup) vegetable oil
3 teaspoons finely chopped dill
150 g (51/2 oz) gravlax or smoked
  salmon
30 small slices pumpernickel

Whisk together the egg yolk, mustard, lemon juice, sugar and 1/2 teaspoon of salt in a bowl. Mix the oils together in a jug and slowly pour into the egg yolk mixture, whisking continuously until all the oil is incorporated and the dressing thickens. Fold through the finely chopped dill and set aside.

Divide the gravlax or salmon between the sliced bread and spoon a little of the dressing over. Season with freshly ground black pepper and serve.

salt and pepper tofu serves 6-8

1 egg white
2 garlic cloves, crushed
1 teaspoon grated fresh ginger
500 g (1 lb 2 oz) firm tofu, cut into
    2 cm (3/4 inch) cubes
3 tablespoons sugar
2 teaspoons lime juice
1 teaspoon finely chopped red chilli
45 g (1 1/2 oz/1/4 cup) finely diced
    cucumber
2 tablespoons finely chopped coriander
    (cilantro) leaves
60 g (2 1/4 oz/1/2 cup) cornflour
    (cornstarch)
1 tablespoon ground sichuan
    peppercorns
1 teaspoon caster (superfine) sugar
1 small red chilli, extra, seeded and
    finely chopped
1 tablespoon sea salt
1 teaspoon freshly ground black
    pepper
1 teaspoon freshly ground white
    pepper
300 ml (10 1/2 fl oz) peanut oil, for frying

Whisk the egg white, then add the garlic, ginger and tofu. Stir to coat the tofu. Cover and refrigerate overnight.

To make a cucumber sauce, put the sugar and 4 tablespoons of water in a small saucepan and bring to the boil. Cool, then add the lime juice, chilli, cucumber and coriander. Set aside.

In a shallow bowl, mix together the cornflour, sichuan pepper, sugar, chilli, sea salt, and black pepper and white pepper.

Heat the oil in a deep frying pan or saucepan over medium heat. Coat the tofu in the flour mixture and shake off any excess. Deep-fry in batches for about 1 minute, or until the tofu is lightly coloured. Drain on paper towels. Repeat with the remaining tofu. Serve accompanied by the cucumber sauce.

taramasalata

4 thick slices of sourdough bread
100 g (3¹/₂ oz) tin tarama (sea mullet
  roe)
1 garlic clove, crushed
1 tablespoon diced red onion
3 tablespoons lemon juice
250 ml (9 fl oz/1 cup) vegetable oil
pitta bread, to serve

Soak the sourdough bread in water. Squeeze any excess moisture from the bread and tear it into pieces. Put the bread into a food processor with the tarama, garlic, onion and lemon juice. Process until smooth and then slowly drizzle in the vegetable oil until it thickens to the consistency of sour cream. Serve with warm pitta bread.

spiced pan bread

125 ml (4 fl oz/1/2 cup) olive oil

2 garlic cloves, roughly chopped

65 g (21/4 oz/1 cup) sliced spring onions (scallions)

1 teaspoon ground cumin

1 handful flat-leaf (Italian) parsley

1 tablespoon roughly grated fresh ginger

1/2 roasted red capsicum (pepper), skin and seeds removed

1 teaspoon seeded and finely chopped red chilli

250 g (9 oz/2 cups) plain (all-purpose) flour

2 teaspoons baking powder

2 tablespoons peanut oil

Put 1 teaspoon of sea salt, the oil, garlic, spring onions, cumin, parsley, ginger, capsicum and chilli in a food processor and blend to form a smooth paste. Set aside. Sift the flour and baking powder into the bowl of a mixer. With the machine running on a low speed, add 4 tablespoons each of hot and cold water. As soon as the dough comes together, transfer to a bowl, cover with plastic wrap and allow to rest for 15 minutes.

Divide the dough into four pieces. Roll out one piece to form a 20 cm (8 in) round. Brush the surface with 2 tablespoons of the spicy paste, roll up into a log then form into a spiral. Tuck the tail end under and flatten the bread. Repeat this process with the remaining dough. Roll out one of the spirals to form a thin 20 cm (8 in) circle. Heat a teaspoon of oil in a frying pan. Cook over medium heat for 4 minutes, or until the bottom is golden. Flip and fry the other side. Drain on paper towels. Roll and fry the remaining pieces of dough. Serve warm, cut into triangles.

sweet potato crisps with baba ghanoush

serves 6

2 tablespoons olive oil

1 garlic bulb, sliced in half horizontally

1 large eggplant (aubergine)

90 g (3 1/4 oz/1/3 cup) tahini

3 tablespoons lemon juice

1 handful finely chopped flat-leaf (Italian) parsley

1 large orange sweet potato

500 ml (17 fl oz/2 cups) vegetable oil

1 teaspoon sumac

Preheat the oven to 200°C (400°F/ Gas 6). Put the olive oil in a baking dish. Place each garlic half, cut side down, on the dish, and add the whole eggplant. Bake for 35–40 minutes, or until the cloves are golden brown and the eggplant is soft. Remove from the oven and allow to cool, then squeeze the flesh from the roasted garlic and put in a blender or food processor. Cut the eggplant in half, scoop out the flesh and add it to the garlic. Blend until smooth. Transfer to a bowl and fold in the tahini. Add the lemon juice, and add salt according to taste. Fold through the parsley and set aside.

Slice the sweet potato very thinly with a sharp knife or vegetable peeler. Heat the oil in a deep frying pan over moderate heat and deep-fry the sweet potato slices, a few at a time, until they are crisp and golden. Drain on paper towels. Sprinkle with sumac and sea salt and serve with baba ghanoush.

roast vegetables
with rouille

serves 4

a selection of vegetables such as
   parsnips, onions, fennel, carrots,
   zucchini (courgette), pumpkin (winter
   squash) and sweet potato
4 tablespoons olive oil
1 thick slice sourdough bread
10 saffron threads
1 red capsicum (pepper), roasted and
   skinned
1/4 teaspoon ground paprika
1 garlic clove
125 ml (4 fl oz/1/2 cup) light olive oil

Preheat the oven to 200°C (400°F/ Gas 6). Cut the vegetables into large chunks. Put into a baking dish and rub with the olive oil. Cover with foil and bake for 1 hour.

To make the rouille, tear the bread into pieces and put in a bowl. Bring the saffron threads and 3 tablespoons of water to the boil in a small saucepan and simmer for 1 minute. Soak the bread in the hot saffron water then add it to a food processor or blender with the capsicum, paprika and garlic. Blend to form a smooth paste. Add the light olive oil in a steady stream.

To serve, arrange the vegetables on a serving plate with the rouille.

spiced red cabbage　　serves 4

2 tablespoons light olive oil
2 garlic cloves, crushed
1 teaspoon fennel seeds
1 tablespoon mustard seeds
500 g (1 lb 2 oz) red cabbage, thinly
　sliced
125 ml (4 fl oz/1/2 cup) red wine

Heat the oil in a deep frying pan over medium heat and add the garlic, fennel seeds and mustard seeds. As the mustard seeds begin to pop, add the cabbage and sauté for a minute. Add the red wine, then cover and simmer over low heat for 30 minutes. Serve with pork loin, or with any roast meat.

fennel salad

2 tablespoons balsamic vinegar
4 tablespoons olive oil
1 teaspoon dijon mustard
2 fennel bulbs, finely sliced
2 oranges, segmented
1 large handful flat-leaf (Italian) parsley
30 g (1 oz/¼ cup) walnuts, roughly
  chopped
20 niçoise olives

Put the vinegar, oil and mustard in a small bowl and stir to combine. Toss the fennel, orange, parsley, walnuts and olives together in a large serving bowl and drizzle with the dressing.

burghul salad

150 g (5¹/₂ oz) burghul (bulgur)
60 g (2¹/₄ oz) currants
2 tablespoons olive oil
2 large red onions, finely chopped
¹/₂ teaspoon ground cinnamon
¹/₂ teaspoon ground cardamom
1 teaspoon allspice
1 tablespoon grated fresh ginger
2 celery sticks, finely sliced
1 red chilli, seeded and finely sliced
200 g (7 oz) cooked chickpeas
60 g (2¹/₄ oz) pine nuts, toasted
1 handful coriander (cilantro) leaves
1 handful flat-leaf (Italian) parsley
10 mint leaves, roughly chopped

Put the burghul and currants into a bowl and cover with 250 ml (9 fl oz/ 1 cup) of boiling water. Heat the olive oil in a large saucepan over medium heat. Add the onion, cinnamon, cardamom, allspice and ginger and cook until the onion is soft. Add the celery, chilli, chickpeas and pine nuts to the soaked burghul and currants. Lightly fold the ingredients together in a bowl. Season with sea salt and freshly ground black pepper.

Spoon into a serving bowl and add the fresh herbs. Serve as a light salad or with grilled chicken.

roast beetroot salad serves 4

4 large beetroot (beets)
2 Lebanese (short) cucumbers,
  julienned
1/2 red onion, finely diced
2 tablespoons finely chopped dill
125 g (41/2 oz/1/2 cup) light sour cream
2 tablespoons grated fresh horseradish
1 tablespoon lemon juice
400 g (14 oz) watercress, broken into
  sprigs

Preheat the oven to 180°C (350°F/ Gas 4). Put the unpeeled beetroot in a roasting tin with 250 ml (9 fl oz/ 1 cup) of water. Cover the tin with foil and bake for 1 hour, or until a knife will pass easily through the beetroot. Remove the beetroot and allow to cool. Put the cucumber in a small bowl with the onion and dill and mix together.

In a separate bowl, combine the sour cream with the horseradish and lemon juice and season to taste.

Peel the skins from the beetroot — they should slip free. Wear rubber gloves while doing this in case you need to rub the skins off. Cut the beetroot into thin slices.

Arrange the beetroot on a serving platter. Top with the cucumber salad and watercress, gently pour over the horseradish dressing, then season and serve.

papaya and coconut sambal

2 teaspoons vegetable oil
1 small onion, finely diced
2 tablespoons finely sliced lemon
    grass, white part only
2 teaspoons sambal oelek
45 g (1½ oz oz/½ cup) desiccated
    coconut, toasted
2 teaspoons soft brown sugar
papaya, to serve

Heat the oil in a frying pan over medium heat and cook the onion, lemon grass and sambal oelek for 5 minutes, stirring occasionally. Reduce the heat to low and add the coconut, ½ teaspoon of salt and the sugar and cook, stirring regularly, for 12–15 minutes, or until golden and crisp. Remove from the heat and allow to cool.

Put the mixture in a food processor and process until mixture resembles breadcrumbs. To serve, slice the papaya into thin wedges and sprinkle with the sambal.

Note – Excess coconut sambal may be stored in an airtight container until ready to use.

warm banana chilli salad

serves 4

8 banana chillies
4 tablespoons extra virgin olive oil
1 tablespoon balsamic vinegar
1 teaspoon ground cumin
400 g (14 oz) flat green beans
10 large black olives, pitted and
   roughly torn
10 basil leaves, torn

Preheat the oven to 180°C (350°F/ Gas 4). Put the banana chillies on a baking tray and bake for 30 minutes, or until the skin begins to blister. To make the dressing, put the extra virgin olive oil, vinegar and cumin in a small bowl and stir to combine. Blanch the beans in boiling salted water for 2 minutes, or until they turn bright green. Drain and rinse under cold running water.

To serve, cross two of the baked chillies on a plate. Top with the beans, olives and basil. Drizzle with the dressing.

puy lentil and spinach salad

200 g (7 oz/1 cup) puy lentils
1 teaspoon sea salt
2 oranges
1 tablespoon balsamic vinegar
4 tablespoons extra virgin olive oil
1 tablespoon dijon mustard
100 g (3¹/₂ oz) baby English spinach
  leaves
8 red radishes, washed and finely
  sliced

Put the lentils in a saucepan with 1 litre (35 fl oz/4 cups) of water and the sea salt, bring to the boil, reduce the heat and simmer for 30 minutes. Put the juice and finely grated zest of 1 orange in a large bowl. Add the vinegar, olive oil and mustard and stir to combine. When the lentils are tender, drain them of any excess water and add to the bowl. Season to taste with sea salt and freshly ground black pepper.

Slice the skin from the remaining orange and cut away the segments. Arrange the spinach leaves, radish and orange segments in a serving bowl, then spoon over the lentils. Garnish with extra orange zest.

fattoush

serves 4

1 garlic clove, crushed
1 teaspoon sea salt
4 tablespoons lemon juice
4 tablespoons extra virgin olive oil
3 ripe tomatoes, cut into wedges
2 tablespoons sumac
1¹/₂ pitta breads
125 ml (4 fl oz/¹/₂ cup) light olive oil
1 telegraph (long) cucumber, peeled,
   seeded, halved and thickly sliced
5 spring onions (scallions), thinly sliced
   at an angle
6 red radishes, thinly sliced
1 handful baby rocket (arugula) leaves
1 handful flat-leaf (Italian) parsley
10 mint leaves, roughly chopped
1 cos (romaine) lettuce, roughly
   chopped

Put the garlic, salt, lemon juice and olive oil in a bowl with the tomatoes and sumac and stir together. Slice or tear the pitta bread into bite-sized pieces and fry in the olive oil over medium heat until golden brown. Remove the fried bread pieces with a slotted spoon. Drain on paper towels. Add the chopped cucumber, spring onions, radishes, rocket, herbs and lettuce to the bowl of tomatoes. Toss the fried bread through the fattoush just before serving.

spiced potatoes

4 tablespoons olive oil

500 g (1 lb 2 oz) all-purpose potatoes, peeled and diced

2 large red chillies, seeded and finely chopped

3 garlic cloves, crushed

1 teaspoon ground cumin

1/2 teaspoon ground coriander

1/2 teaspoon paprika

lime wedges, to serve

2 tablespoons lime juice

1 handful coriander (cilantro) leaves

Heat the olive oil in a heavy-based frying pan over medium heat. Add the potatoes to the oil and stir to coat well. Add the chillies, garlic, spices and some salt to taste.

Stir the potatoes carefully around the pan until they are soft and golden. Put them on a serving platter with lime wedges, spoon the lime juice over the potatoes and garnish with the coriander leaves.

rice with vermicelli, parsley and puy lentils

serves 4

100 ml (3¹/2 fl oz) olive oil
3 garlic cloves, crushed
3 red onions, finely sliced
2 teaspoons ground cumin
1 egg vermicelli nest
250 g (9 oz) basmati rice
100 g (3¹/2 oz) puy lentils
1 handful flat-leaf (Italian) parsley,
   roughly chopped
tahini sauce (basics), to serve

Heat 2 tablespoons of the olive oil in a frying pan and add the garlic, onions and cumin. Cook over medium heat, stirring occasionally, until the onions are dark brown and caramelized. Heat the remaining 3 tablespoons of oil in a large saucepan over medium heat. Crush the vermicelli nest in your hands and add to the oil. Stir until the noodles are golden, then add the rice and lentils. Stir together before adding 800 ml (28 fl oz) of water and a heaped teaspoon of sea salt. Bring to the boil then reduce the heat to low, cover with a lid and simmer for 20 minutes, or until the water is absorbed. Stir in the caramelized onions and spoon into a serving bowl. Garnish with the parsley and serve with the tahini sauce. Serve with roast chicken or spicy sausages.

eggy crepe roll-up   makes 10

sweet pepper filling
1 tablespoon olive oil
2 teaspoons ground cumin
1 teaspoon ground coriander
2 teaspoons mustard seeds
2 red onions, diced
2 garlic cloves, finely chopped
1 red capsicum (pepper), diced
1 yellow capsicum (pepper), diced
1 tablespoon balsamic vinegar

crepes
20 g (3/4 oz/1/3 cup) finely sliced chives
1 quantity crepe mixture (basics)
50 g (13/4 oz) butter, softened
2 handfuls finely chopped coriander
   (cilantro) leaves

Heat the oil in a frying pan over high heat and add the cumin, coriander and mustard seeds. When the mustard seeds begin to pop, add the onion and garlic. Reduce the heat and continue to cook for 5–7 minutes, stirring occasionally, until the onion is transparent. Add the capsicum, cover and cook for a further 15 minutes, stirring occasionally. Add the vinegar and season with salt and freshly ground black pepper.

Stir the chives through the crepe batter. Grease a small frying pan with a little butter and place over medium heat. Add 2 tablespoons of batter and swirl the pan around until the mixture coats the surface. Cook for a few minutes until the edges are crisp, then turn and cook the other side for a further minute. Remove from the pan and repeat with the remaining batter. When all the crepes are cooked, place a heaped tablespoon of the filling along the centre of each one, sprinkle with coriander and roll up.

steamed eggplant salad

serves 4

65 g (2¹/4 oz/¹/4 cup) tahini
60 g (2¹/4 oz/¹/4 cup) plain yoghurt
2 tablespoons lemon juice
2 teaspoons ground cumin
1 garlic clove, minced
2 eggplants (aubergines)
40 g (1¹/2 oz/¹/4 cup) toasted pine nuts
1 handful coriander (cilantro) leaves
1–2 tablespoons extra virgin olive oil
1 teaspoon smoked paprika

To make the dressing, put the tahini, yoghurt, lemon juice, cumin and garlic into a bowl. Add 3 tablespoons of water and stir until smooth. Set aside. Trim the ends off the eggplant. Thinly slice, widthways, and place into a steamer. Season with a little sea salt and freshly ground black pepper. Steam for 5–7 minutes, or until the eggplants are soft. Arrange on a serving plate, drizzle with the dressing and scatter with the pine nuts and coriander. Drizzle with the extra virgin olive oil and sprinkle with the paprika.

coconut spiced sweet potato

serves 4

600 g (1 lb 5 oz) sweet potato, peeled
  and cut into bite-sized pieces
1 small cinnamon stick
2 large red chillies, seeded and
  finely sliced
finely grated zest of 1 orange
1/2 teaspoon ground nutmeg
400 ml (14 fl oz) coconut milk
buttered couscous (basics)
80 g (2 3/4 oz) coriander (cilantro) sprigs
1/2 teaspoon smoked paprika

Put the sweet potato, cinnamon, chillies, orange zest, nutmeg and coconut milk in a saucepan with 250 ml (9 fl oz/1 cup) of water. Bring to the boil and then reduce the heat to a simmer. Cook for 30 minutes, or until the sweet potato is soft and cooked through. Serve on a bed of buttered couscous. Garnish with coriander sprigs and a sprinkle of paprika. Serve with chicken or pork.

rocket with baked
saffron ricotta

serves 4

500 g (1 lb 2 oz/2 cups) ricotta cheese
pinch of saffron threads
2 tablespoons olive oil
1 teaspoon balsamic vinegar
3 teaspoons walnut oil
2 fennel bulbs, thinly sliced
300 g (10½ oz) rocket (arugula),
  stalks removed

Preheat the oven to 180°C (350°F/ Gas 4). Put the ricotta cheese in an ovenproof dish lined with baking paper. Sprinkle with saffron, drizzle with olive oil and season with sea salt and freshly ground black pepper. Bake for 30 minutes. Remove from the oven and allow to cool.

Combine the vinegar and walnut oil in a bowl and add the fennel and rocket leaves. Toss together and serve with the baked ricotta.

rice with tomatoes and spinach

serves 6

20 g (³/₄ oz) butter
500 g (1 lb 2 oz) English spinach,
   washed and drained
400 g (14 oz/2 cups) basmati rice
3 tablespoons light olive oil
¹/₂ teaspoon ground turmeric
1 teaspoon ground cumin
1 red onion, finely sliced
2 vine-ripened tomatoes, finely
   chopped
750 ml (26 fl oz/3 cups) vegetable
   stock

Melt the butter in a frying pan over medium heat. Finely chop the spinach and add it to the hot butter. Cover and cook until the spinach is dark green and softly wilted. Remove and set aside. Wash the rice several times until the water runs clear.

In a large saucepan, heat the olive oil over medium heat and add the turmeric, cumin and onion. Continue to cook for 5–7 minutes, or until the onion is golden and slightly caramelized. Add the rice and stir together for 1 minute. Squeeze any excess moisture from the spinach then add it to the rice along with the tomatoes and stock. Stir once, then bring to the boil. Cover, reduce the heat to low, and cook for 25 minutes. Serve with yoghurt, grilled (broiled) fish and a wedge of fresh lime.

coconut and ginger pancakes with five-spice duck

makes 20

1 Chinese barbecued duck, skin and flesh shredded
2 teaspoons Chinese five-spice
175 g (6 oz/1 cup) rice flour
435 ml (15¼ fl oz/1¾ cups) coconut milk
1 egg, beaten
1 tablespoon shaved palm sugar (jaggery)
1 teaspoon grated fresh ginger
1–2 tablespoons peanut oil
2 handfuls coriander (cilantro) leaves
hoisin or plum sauce

Place the duck skin on a baking tray and grill (broil) for 1–2 minutes, or until crisp. Place in a bowl. Add the shredded duck meat and any meat juices. Stir in the five-spice powder. Make the pancakes by sifting the rice flour and ¼ teaspoon of salt into a bowl. Make a well in the centre and stir in the coconut milk, egg, sugar and ginger. Whisk to form a smooth batter. Heat the oil in a frying pan over high heat. Place 2–3 coriander leaves in the centre and drizzle 2 tablespoons of the batter over them to form a pancake 10 cm (4 in) in diameter. Cook until the edges start to go crisp. Turn and cook the other side. Repeat with the remaining batter. Place some of the duck mix along one end of each pancake and top with a little hoisin or plum sauce. Roll up and serve.

crab tartlets lentil and fennel sausage salad vietnamese beef soup spicy vegetables with couscous tomato and tofu broth saffron mash with roast beets and mushrooms eggplant and tofu salad squid salad with red capsicum and curry vinaigrette braised beef with shiitake mushrooms beetroot and goat's cheese salad ginger duck and udon noodle broth farmhouse cheese with pomegranate and radicchio tamarind duck

02 light meals

salad tofu with a black bean sauce wild rice kedgeree red lentil soup eggplant relish with chicken saffron squid and chive salad seared beef slices with plum sauce and mint salad fish and saffron broth skewered swordfish with a spiced

crab tartlets

serves 6

250 g (9 oz) cherry tomatoes
1 teaspoon chopped thyme
10 saffron threads
150 ml (5 fl oz) cream (whipping)
2 egg yolks
2 tablespoons finely chopped chives
6 pre-baked 8 cm (3¼ in) shortcrust
  tartlet cases (basics)
150 g (5½ oz) crab meat
bitter leaf salad, to serve

Preheat the oven to 180°C (350°F/ Gas 4). Put the cherry tomatoes and thyme in a small baking dish and bake for 20 minutes, or until the tomatoes are beginning to split.

Meanwhile, heat the saffron threads with 4 tablespoons of water in a small saucepan over high heat until the liquid has reduced to 1 tablespoon. Put the saffron liquid in a bowl with the cream, egg yolks and chives then whisk together. Remove the cherry tomatoes from the oven and roughly chop, discarding any tough pieces of skin. Spoon the tomato mixture into the base of the tartlets and then divide the crab meat between them. Ladle the cream mixture into the tart cases. Bake for 15 minutes, or until they are just set. Serve with a bitter leaf salad.

tomato and tofu broth

serves 4

1 litre (35 fl oz/4 cups) dashi stock
  (basics)
2 teaspoons mirin
4 tablespoons white miso paste
1 tablespoon grated fresh ginger
4 roma (plum) tomatoes
300 g (10 1/2 oz) silken firm tofu
120 g (4 1/4 oz) baby English spinach
  leaves
1 tablespoon soy sauce

Put the dashi stock, mirin, white miso paste and ginger in a saucepan and bring to the boil, then reduce the heat to a gentle simmer.

Slice the tomatoes in half and scoop out the seeds using a spoon. Discard the seeds, dice the tomato flesh and add the tomatoes to the broth, simmering for a further 10 minutes.

Cut the tofu into cubes and put it into four soup bowls. Add the spinach leaves and soy sauce to the broth and cook for 1 minute, or until the leaves have just wilted. Ladle the soup over the tofu and serve immediately.

eggplant and tofu salad

2 tablespoons white miso paste
1 tablespoon soy sauce
1 tablespoon sugar
1 tablespoon sesame oil
3 tablespoons oil
1 tablespoon finely grated fresh ginger
6 Japanese eggplants (aubergines), cut into chunks
2 red banana chillies, seeded and cut into rings
2 green banana chillies, seeded and cut into rings
400 g (14 oz) smoked tofu, cut into cubes
1 spring onion (scallion), finely chopped
1 tablespoon toasted sesame seeds

Mix the miso, soy sauce and sugar together while slowly adding 250 ml (9 fl oz/1 cup) of water.

Heat both the oils together in a large frying pan or wok and add the ginger. As the ginger begins to sizzle, add the eggplant and toss until it is golden brown, then pour in the miso and soy mixture and simmer for 10 minutes. Add the banana chillies and cook for a further 2 minutes, or until they are just beginning to soften.

Divide the tofu between four plates, top with the eggplant and garnish with the spring onion and sesame seeds.

farmhouse cheese with pomegranate and radicchio

serves 4

2 tablespoons oil
1 tablespoon brown mustard seeds
1 teaspoon ground cumin
1 red capsicum (pepper), thinly
   julienned
1 yellow capsicum (pepper), thinly
   julienned
1 teaspoon sugar
1 small radicchio, leaves washed
200 g (7 oz) fresh farmhouse cheese or
   goat's curd
1 pomegranate, seeds separated out
   and juice reserved

Heat the oil in a large frying pan over high heat and add the mustard seeds and ground cumin. As the seeds begin to pop, add the capsicum and sugar. Toss until the capsicum is beginning to soften and then remove the pan from the heat.

To serve, make a bed of the radicchio leaves on a plate and top them with the capsicum. Add a scoop of the cheese and the pomegranate seeds before drizzling with any pomegranate juice. Season well.

braised beef with shiitake mushrooms

12 dried shiitake mushrooms
2 garlic cloves, peeled
2 star anise
1 large red chilli, seeded and roughly
  chopped
3 cm (1 1/4 in) piece fresh ginger, peeled
  and thickly sliced
1 daikon, peeled and cut into 1 cm
  (1/2 in) thick slices
2 carrots, peeled and sliced
4 x 150 g (5 1/2 oz) beef fillet pieces
3 tablespoons soy sauce
3 tablespoons mirin
6 spring onions (scallions), sliced into
  2 cm (3/4 in) lengths
4 small zucchini (courgettes), cut
  diagonally into thick slices

Put the shiitake mushrooms into a large bowl and cover with 1 litre (35 fl oz/ 4 cups) of hot water. Weight the mushrooms down with a small plate so they remain covered by the water rather than floating to the surface. Soak for 30 minutes before removing the mushrooms from the water and straining the liquid in a large saucepan. Trim the mushrooms of any coarse stalks and put them in the saucepan with the garlic, star anise, chilli, ginger, daikon and carrot. Bring to the boil then reduce the heat to a simmer and cook for 10 minutes. Add the beef, soy sauce and mirin. Cover with a lid and continue to simmer slowly for a further 30 minutes. Add the spring onions and zucchini and cook for a further 5 minutes.

Serve with the vegetables spooned over the beef, surrounded by a pool of the cooking liquid, and a bowl of creamy mashed potato or steamed rice on the side.

squid salad with red capsicum and curry vinaigrette serves 4

2 red capsicums (peppers)
10 large basil leaves, roughly torn
1 tablespoon lemon juice
1 teaspoon brown sugar
1 teaspoon curry powder
5 tablespoons extra virgin olive oil
500 g (1 lb 2 oz) small squid, cleaned
100 g (3½ oz) baby English spinach
  leaves

Preheat the oven to 200°C (400°F/ Gas 6). Roast the capsicums in the oven, then put in a plastic bag or covered bowl and allow to cool. When they have cooled, peel away the skin, take out the seeds and finely slice the flesh. Put the sliced capsicum in a large bowl with the basil leaves. Blend together the lemon juice, brown sugar, curry powder and 4 tablespoons of the olive oil and pour over the capsicum. Season to taste.

Heat a large frying pan over high heat, add the remaining olive oil and sear the squid for 2 minutes on each side or until it is cooked. Slice the squid into thick rings before adding it to the capsicum. Toss the spinach leaves through the salad and season to taste.

tofu with a
black bean sauce

serves 4

2 tablespoons olive oil
1 tablespoon finely grated fresh ginger
2 garlic cloves, minced
1 teaspoon chilli powder
2 tablespoons salted black beans,
   rinsed and drained
3 tablespoons mirin
400 g (14 oz) hard tofu, cut into 2 cm
   (3/4 in) squares
6 zucchini (courgettes), trimmed and
   finely sliced on the diagonal
1 lemon, juiced
steamed rice, to serve

Put the olive oil in a large frying pan or wok and heat over high heat. Add the ginger, garlic and chilli powder and stir-fry for 1 minute. Add the black beans, mirin and 125 ml (4 fl oz/ 1/2 cup) of water. Reduce the heat to a simmer, then add the tofu and season with black pepper. Cook for 5 minutes, then add the zucchini. Toss together and cook for a further 2 minutes before adding the lemon juice. Serve with steamed rice.

vietnamese beef soup serves 4

2 litres (70 fl oz/8 cups) beef stock
1 lemon grass stem, crushed
1/4 teaspoon Chinese five-spice
1 tablespoon finely grated fresh ginger
2 red onions, peeled and finely sliced
180 g (6 oz) dried rice vermicelli
400 g (14 oz) rump steak, semi-frozen
   and thinly sliced
3 tablespoons fish sauce
80 g (2 3/4 oz) mint
90 g (3 1/4 oz) coriander (cilantro) leaves
50 g (1 3/4 oz) Vietnamese mint

Put the stock, lemon grass, five-spice powder, ginger and onion in a large saucepan over high heat and bring to the boil. Reduce the heat and simmer for 10 minutes. Place the rice vermicelli in a large bowl and cover with boiling water. Soak for 5 minutes, then drain and set aside.

Add the steak and fish sauce to the soup and simmer for 1 minute. Divide the noodles between four bowls then ladle over the hot soup, removing the lemon grass stalk. Add a handful of mixed herbs to each bowl and serve.

saffron mash with roast beets and mushrooms
serves 4

8 baby beetroots (beets)

300 g (10½ oz) mixed pine, oyster and
   fresh shiitake mushrooms

3 tablespoons extra virgin olive oil

2 garlic cloves, finely sliced

8 thyme sprigs

1 kg (2 lb 4 oz) all-purpose potatoes,
   peeled and cut into chunks

125 ml (4 fl oz/½ cup) milk

15 saffron threads

100 g (3½ oz) butter

4 tablespoons toasted pumpkin seeds
   (pepitas)

Preheat the oven to 200°C (400°F/ Gas 6). Put the beetroots in a baking dish with 125 ml (4 fl oz/½ cup) of water. Cover with foil and bake for 1 hour, or until cooked. Rub the skin off the cooked beetroots then slice in half and wrap in foil. Bake the mushrooms with olive oil, garlic and thyme in a baking dish covered with foil for 30 minutes. Just prior to serving, return the mushrooms and beetroots to the oven to warm.

Meanwhile, cook the potatoes in a saucepan of salted water and drain. Heat the milk, saffron and butter in a saucepan over medium–low heat until the saffron begins to colour the milk. Mash the potatoes while still warm then whisk in the saffron milk. Season with sea salt. Cut the warmed beetroot into quarters and serve with the mash and mushrooms. Sprinkle with toasted pumpkin seeds and thyme sprigs from the baking dish.

red lentil soup

3 tablespoons olive oil

1 onion, finely diced

1 tablespoon grated fresh ginger

1 tablespoon ground cumin

2 carrots, peeled and grated

250 g (9 oz/1 cup) red lentils

1 litre (35 fl oz/4 cups) vegetable stock
  (basics) or water

2 red onions, finely sliced

80 g (2³/₄ oz) coriander (cilantro) sprigs,
  with roots attached

Put 1 tablespoon of olive oil into a large saucepan and add the onion, ginger and cumin. Cook over medium heat until the onion is soft and transparent. Add the carrot, lentils and stock. Bring the soup to the boil then reduce to a simmer. Cook for 30 minutes, or until the lentils have completely disintegrated.

Meanwhile, heat the remaining olive oil in a frying pan over medium heat and add the red onions. Thoroughly wash the coriander. Finely chop the roots and stems, leaving the top leafy section for garnishing later. Add the chopped coriander roots and stems to the red onion and continue to cook, stirring occasionally, until the onions are caramelized.

To serve, ladle the soup into bowls, garnish with a sprinkling of coriander leaves then top with a spoonful of the caramelized onions.

wild rice kedgeree   serves 4

190 g (6³/₄ oz/1 cup) wild rice
400 g (14 oz) salmon fillet

curry sauce
60 g (2¹/₄ oz) butter
1 red onion, finely diced
1 garlic clove, crushed
2 teaspoons grated fresh ginger
1 teaspoon ground turmeric
1 teaspoon ground cumin
10 saffron threads
1 tablespoon tomato paste
  (concentrated purée)
250 ml (9 fl oz/1 cup) white wine

1 lemon, halved for squeezing
1 handful flat-leaf (Italian) parsley
1 handful coriander (cilantro) leaves
2 vine-ripened tomatoes, cut into
  eighths
4 eggs, soft boiled, cut into quarters

Preheat the oven to 180°C (350°F/ Gas 4). Wash the rice in cold water and put in a saucepan. Cover with 1.5 litres (52 fl oz/6 cups) of water and a pinch of sea salt. Bring to the boil then simmer for about 25 minutes, drain, fluff with a fork and set aside.

Slice the salmon into 4 pieces and put in a shallow pan or baking tray. Bake for 5 minutes.

Meanwhile, to make the curry sauce, melt the butter in a heavy-based frying pan and fry the onion, garlic and ginger until the onion is soft and transparent. Add all the spices and fry for a further minute. Add the tomato paste and white wine and allow to simmer until it has reduced by half.

Remove the salmon and squeeze the lemon over the top before breaking up the salmon into pieces. To assemble, toss the rice with half the herbs and a little of the curry sauce and arrange on plates. Top with the tomatoes, egg quarters, salmon, remaining herbs and a drizzle of the sauce.

ginger duck and
udon noodle broth   serves 4

8 dried shiitake mushrooms

2 duck breast fillets

8 spring onions (scallions), trimmed
   and sliced into 2 cm (3/4 in) lengths

2 tablespoons finely grated fresh ginger

200 g (7 oz) udon noodles

1 tablespoon dashi granules

4 tablespoons soy sauce

1 tablespoon sugar

200 g (7 oz) silken firm tofu, cut into
   2 cm (3/4 in) cubes

2 tablespoons finely chopped garlic
   chives

Bring a saucepan of salted water to the boil. Put the mushrooms in a bowl and cover with warm water. Soak for 10 minutes then remove the stalks and finely slice. Return the mushrooms to their soaking liquid. Trim the fatty skin from the duck and reserve. Cut the breast diagonally in thin slices. Heat the duck fat in a frying pan over medium heat. Add the shallots, duck and ginger and sauté lightly for 4–5 minutes. Set aside and discard any fat.

Cook the noodles in the boiling water until *al dente* then drain and rinse. Combine the dashi granules, soy sauce, sugar and 1.25 litres (44 fl oz/ 5 cups) of water in a saucepan and bring to the boil. Reduce the heat, add the mushrooms and their strained soaking liquid. Simmer for 10 minutes. Add the duck, shallots, ginger and tofu. Cook for 1 minute. Divide the noodles between 4 bowls, ladle over the broth and sprinkle with chives.

beetroot and
goat's cheese salad   serves 4-6

4 large beetroot (beets)
400 g (14 oz) butternut pumpkin
  (squash), cut into bite-sized chunks
3 tablespoons olive oil
75 g (2^1/$_2$ oz/^{1}/$_2$ cup) hazelnuts
1 tablespoon balsamic vinegar
1 teaspoon brown mustard seeds
240 g (8^1/$_2$ oz) rocket (arugula)
200 g (7 oz) goat's cheese

Preheat the oven to 180°C (350°F/ Gas 4). Put the unpeeled beetroot into a roasting tin with 250 ml (9 fl oz/ 1 cup) of water. Cover the tin with foil and bake for 1 hour, or until a knife will pass easily through the beetroot. Remove the beetroot. Allow to cool.

Toss the pumpkin in 2 tablespoons of the olive oil, season well and roast for 15 minutes, or until it is pale brown and cooked through. Roast the hazelnuts for 5 minutes. Allow to cool before rubbing away their skins.

Peel the skins from the beetroot — they should simply slip free. Wear rubber gloves in case you need to rub the skins off. Slice the beetroot into eighths lengthways.

Mix the vinegar, remaining olive oil and mustard seeds. Put the beetroot, pumpkin, hazelnuts and rocket in a bowl, toss with the dressing and season. Serve salad in a bowl with the goat's cheese crumbled over.

tamarind duck salad   serves 4

4 duck breasts, thinly sliced across
   the grain
125 ml (4 fl oz/1/2 cup) tamarind water
   (basics)
2 tablespoons grated fresh ginger
1 teaspoon Chinese five-spice
2 tablespoons shaved palm sugar
   (jaggery)
115 g (4 oz) snow peas (mangetout)
1 tablespoon sesame oil
1 red capsicum (pepper), julienned
115 g (4 oz) bean sprouts, trimmed
2 tablespoons sesame seeds, toasted

Put the sliced duck breasts, tamarind water, ginger, five-spice and palm sugar in a bowl and leave to marinate for at least 30 minutes.

Blanch the snow peas in boiling water, refresh under cold running water, then slice in half lengthways. Heat a wok over high heat. Swirl the sesame oil around the wok, add the marinated duck. Stir-fry over high heat for 5 minutes, or until the duck is cooked. Remove the duck from the heat and allow it to cool a little before tossing with the snow peas, capsicum and bean sprouts.

Deglaze the wok with the remaining marinade and allow it to simmer for 5 minutes. Pour this over the salad as a dressing and garnish with toasted sesame seeds.

spicy vegetables with couscous

1 red onion, cut into eighths
2 garlic cloves, finely sliced
1 cinnamon stick
2 cm (3/4 in) piece fresh ginger, peeled
  and quartered
1 teaspoon ground paprika
pinch of saffron
400 g (14 oz) tin chopped tomatoes
2 red capsicums (peppers), seeded
  and cut into pieces
1 tablespoon soft brown sugar
400 g (14 oz) cooked chickpeas
3 tablespoons oil
4 Japanese eggplants (aubergines),
  sliced in half lengthways
80 g (2 3/4 oz) coriander (cilantro) sprigs,
  roughly chopped
buttered couscous (basics)

Put the onion, garlic, spices and tomatoes in a large saucepan, pour in 250 ml (9 fl oz/1 cup) of water and bring to the boil. Add the capsicum, sugar and chickpeas, season and simmer for 30 minutes.

Heat the oil in a frying pan over high heat and fry the eggplants until golden and puffy. Drain on paper towels.

Remove the cinnamon and ginger chunks from the tomato sauce and stir in the coriander. Serve the eggplant with the tomato and capsicum sauce and buttered couscous.

saffron squid
and chive salad

serves 4

300 g (10¹/2 oz) orecchiette pasta
3 tablespoons lemon juice
140 ml (4¹/2 fl oz) extra virgin olive oil
30 g (1 oz) chives, chopped into 1 cm
   (¹/2 in) lengths
2 small red chillies, seeded and finely
   chopped
2 tablespoons olive oil
10 saffron threads
1 large red onion, finely diced
6 small squid, cleaned
1 handful flat-leaf (Italian) parsley,
   roughly chopped
2 handfuls baby rocket (arugula) leaves

Bring a large saucepan of salted water to the boil and cook the orecchiette until *al dente*. Drain and set aside.

Meanwhile, put the lemon juice, extra virgin olive oil, chives and chillies into a large bowl and stir to combine.

Heat a large non-stick frying pan over medium heat and add the olive oil and saffron. After 1 minute add the onion and cook until soft and transparent. Remove most of the onion from the pan with a slotted spoon and add it to the dressing in the bowl.

Increase the heat and quickly sauté the squid – they should only need a few minutes on each side. Roughly slice the cooked squid and add to the dressing. Season with sea salt and freshly ground black pepper. Add the pasta and toss together. Pile into a large bowl with the parsley and rocket.

eggplant relish with chicken

4 tablespoons olive oil

10 small Japanese eggplants (aubergines), sliced in half lengthways

4 red onions, finely sliced

4 garlic cloves, finely sliced

3 tablespoons red wine vinegar

4 tablespoons lemon juice

3 tablespoons soft brown sugar

2 teaspoons white peppercorns, lightly crushed

1 handful coriander (cilantro) leaves

4 skinless, boneless chicken breast fillets

Preheat the oven to 200°C (400°F/ Gas 6). Heat the olive oil in a frying pan over medium–high heat. Fry the eggplant until it is golden brown. Remove and put in a large bowl. Add the onions and garlic and, reducing the heat, stir-fry until the onions are soft. Add to the eggplant. Put the vinegar, lemon juice, sugar and peppercorns into a saucepan and heat over medium heat until the sugar has dissolved. Bring to the boil and pour the hot mixture over the eggplant and onion. Stir to combine and add the coriander when the relish is cool.

Meanwhile, heat a large frying pan over high heat and sear the chicken until golden brown on both sides. Transfer to a baking tray and cover with foil. Bake for 15 minutes, or until cooked through. Serve with the eggplant relish on the side.

seared beef slices with plum sauce and mint salad

serves 4

4 tablespoons plum sauce
4 tablespoons olive oil
1 tablespoon balsamic vinegar
1/2 teaspoon ground sichuan
   peppercorns
4 spring onions (scallions), finely sliced
400 g (14 oz) sirloin steak, trimmed
100 g (31/2 oz) bean sprouts, trimmed
1 butter lettuce
80 g (23/4 oz) mint sprigs, leaves picked
2 tablespoons finely chopped cashew
   nuts

Put the plum sauce, olive oil, vinegar, ground sichuan peppercorns and spring onions in a bowl. Stir to combine. Heat a frying pan over high heat and sear the steak for 2 minutes on both sides. Remove from the heat and allow to rest in the pan.

Divide the bean sprouts and butter lettuce between four plates. Top with a scattering of mint leaves. Finely slice the beef and lay it over the salad. Spoon over the plum sauce mixture and sprinkle with the cashews.

fish and saffron broth

10 g (¹/₄ oz) butter
1 large pinch saffron threads
1 onion, finely diced
2 garlic cloves, crushed
1 teaspoon finely grated fresh ginger
30 g (1 oz) fresh ginger, peeled and cut
   into thin strips
6 ripe roma (plum) tomatoes, diced
2 tablespoons tomato paste
   (concentrated purée)
¹/₂ teaspoon sea salt
4 spring onions (scallions), trimmed
   and cut into 3 cm (1¹/₄ in) lengths
8 x 115 g (4 oz) pieces firm white fish,
   such as ling
1 handful coriander (cilantro) leaves
crusty bread, to serve

Put the butter, saffron, onion, garlic and all the ginger into a large heavy-based frying pan and cook over medium heat for 2–3 minutes until the onion becomes translucent. Add 500 ml (17 fl oz/2 cups) of water, the tomatoes, tomato paste and salt and then simmer, covered, for 20 minutes. Put the spring onions and fish pieces into the tomato broth and cook, covered, for 7 minutes.

Divide the fish and broth between four pasta bowls and top with the coriander. Serve with crusty bread.

skewered swordfish with a spiced tahini sauce serves 4

1 red onion
1 tablespoon sea salt
3 lemons
1 teaspoon caster (superfine) sugar
135 g (4³/₄ oz/¹/₂ cup) tahini
2 tablespoons plain yoghurt
1 teaspoon ground cumin
4 swordfish steaks, cut into chunks
3 Lebanese (small) cucumbers, thinly
   sliced on the diagonal

Soak four wooden skewers in water for 1 hour. Cut the onion in half and then finely slice into very thin strips. Put in a bowl and sprinkle with sea salt. Leave for 20 minutes. Rinse the onion under cold water. Squeeze dry and return to the bowl with the juice of 1 lemon and the sugar. Toss to combine.

To make the spiced tahini sauce, combine the tahini with the juice of 1 lemon, yoghurt, cumin and 3 tablespoons of water in a bowl.

Slice the remaining lemon in half and then into thick slices. Thread the swordfish and lemon slices onto the skewers. Season with sea salt and set aside. Toss the cucumber and pickled onion together then divide between four plates. Heat a large non-stick frying pan over medium–high heat and cook each fish skewer for 2 minutes on each side. Serve with the cucumber salad and tahini sauce.

salad of beetroot, chickpea and feta

serves 4

800 g (1 lb 12 oz) beetroot (beets),
  leafy tops removed
1/2 teaspoon ground cumin
1 orange, juiced
2 tablespoons extra virgin olive oil
100 g (3½ oz) wild rocket (arugula)
425 g (15 oz) tin chickpeas, drained
150 g (5½ oz) marinated feta cheese

Preheat the oven to 200°C (400°F/ Gas 6). Put the beetroots into a baking dish with 125 ml (4 fl oz/ 1/2 cup) of water. Cover with foil and bake in the oven for 1 hour, or until cooked through. A sharp knife should pass easily through the beetroot when it is done. Remove and allow to cool. Peel the skins from the beetroot — they should slip free. Wear rubber gloves while doing this in case you need to rub the skins off. Cut the beetroots into small wedges and place in a bowl. Add the ground cumin, orange juice and olive oil and toss to ensure the beetroot is coated in the dressing.

Arrange the rocket, dressed beetroot, chickpeas and marinated feta on a serving dish and drizzle with any of the remaining beetroot dressing.

spiced carrot soup   serves 4

50 g (1¹/₂ oz) butter
1 red onion, diced
1 teaspoon ground cumin
60 g (2¹/₄ oz/¹/₄ cup) red lentils
500 g (1 lb 2 oz) carrots, peeled and
  finely chopped
1 litre (35 fl oz/4 cups) vegetable stock
  (basics)

Put the butter into a saucepan over medium heat and add the onions and cumin. Cook until the onions are soft and transparent, then add the lentils and carrots. Stir for 1 minute, then add the vegetable stock. Bring to the boil, then reduce the heat to a slow simmer. Continue to cook for 40 minutes, or until the carrot is soft and beginning to fall apart. Remove from the heat and allow to cool. Put the soup into a food processor or blender a few ladles at a time, and blend to a smooth purée. Return to a clean saucepan and heat over low heat when ready to serve.

sichuan eggplant

serves 4

250 ml (9 fl oz/1 cup) vegetable oil
2 small eggplants (aubergines), cut into
  pieces
2 large red chillies, seeded and finely
  sliced
1 teaspoon roasted sichuan
  peppercorns, ground
2 garlic cloves, finely chopped
1 1/2 tablespoons finely grated fresh
  ginger
4 spring onions (scallions), sliced
  diagonally
3 tablespoons light soy sauce
1 tablespoon balsamic vinegar
1 teaspoon sugar

Heat the oil in a wok or deep saucepan and deep-fry the eggplant in batches until it is golden brown. Remove the eggplant using a slotted spoon and drain on paper towels. Pour most of the oil out of the wok, leaving behind 1 tablespoon.

Reheat the oil and add the chilli, peppercorns, garlic, ginger and spring onions. Stir-fry for 30 seconds, add the fried eggplant, soy sauce, vinegar and sugar and stir-fry for a further minute. Serve with buckwheat or somen noodles.

roast pumpkin and quinoa salad

serves 4

1 kg (2 lb 4 oz) pumpkin (winter squash) , seeds removed and peeled
2 red capsicums (peppers)
100 g (3¹/2 oz/¹/2 cup) quinoa
2 tablespoons olive oil
100 g (3¹/2 oz) rocket (arugula) leaves
harissa (basics), to serve

Preheat the oven to 180°C (350°F/Gas 4). Cut the pumpkin into 2 cm (³/4 in) thick wedges and place onto a baking tray lined with baking parchment. Rub some of the olive oil over the pumpkin pieces and season with freshly ground black pepper. Cut the capsicums into 2 cm (³/4 in) squares and place onto another lined baking tray. Bake pumpkin and capsicum for 20 minutes. Remove the capsicum. Set aside. Turn each of the pumpkin pieces over, then return to the oven for a further 20 minutes.

Rinse the quinoa in a small strainer under cold running water. Drain and place the grains in a saucepan with 250 ml (9 fl oz/1 cup) of cold water. Bring to the boil. Reduce to a simmer, cover and cook until all the water is absorbed. Drain. Remove the pumpkin from the oven and arrange the pieces between 4 warm plates. Add the rocket leaves and baked capsicum and then spoon over the quinoa. Serve with a dollop of harissa.

mexican spiced chilli beans

serves 4

2 tablespoons olive oil
1 onion, finely diced
2 garlic cloves, crushed
1 1/2 teaspoon smoked paprika
2 teaspoons ground cumin
1/2 teaspoon oregano
500 g (1 lb 2 oz) minced (ground) pork
1 tablespoon tomato paste
   (concentrated purée)
250 ml (9 fl oz/1 cup) red wine
400 g (14 oz) tin chopped tomatoes
400 g (14 oz) tin kidney beans
20 kalamata olives, pitted and roughly
   chopped
coriander (cilantro) leaves, sour cream
   and flat bread, to serve

Put the olive oil in a large saucepan with the chopped onion, garlic, paprika, cumin and oregano. Cook over medium heat until the onion is soft, then add the pork mince. Sauté until the minced pork is cooked through and beginning to break up. Add the tomato paste, red wine, and chopped tomatoes and stir to combine. Simmer over low heat for 40 minutes, then add the kidney beans and olives. Cook for a further 10 minutes before spooning into warm bowls and serving with a garnish of fresh coriander, sour cream and some crisp flat bread.

lentil and fennel sausage salad

200 g (7 oz/1 cup) puy lentils
1 teaspoon sea salt
1 tablespoon balsamic vinegar
4 tablespoons extra virgin olive oil
1 tablespoon wholegrain mustard
8 fennel sausages
1/2 red onion, thinly sliced
50 g (13/4 oz/1 cup) croutons (basics)
1 large handful flat-leaf (Italian) parsley

Put the lentils in a saucepan with 1 litre (35 fl oz/4 cups) of water and the sea salt. Bring to the boil, reduce the heat and simmer for 30 minutes, or until tender. Drain lentils of any excess water. Stir in the vinegar, 2 tablespoons of olive oil and the mustard.

Cook the sausages in a frying pan until they are cooked through.

Toss the red onion, croutons and parsley through the lentils, divide between four plates and drizzle with a little more olive oil. Top with the sausages and serve with a dollop of extra mustard.

thyme and sumac-seared tuna with minted potatoes

serves 4

600 g (1 lb 5 oz) kipfler (fingerling) or new potatoes
1 tablespoon finely chopped thyme
3 tablespoons finely chopped chives
3 tablespoons sumac
500 g (1 lb 2 oz) tuna fillet, cut into smaller fillets
2 tablespoons olive oil
125 ml (4 fl oz/1/2 cup) extra virgin olive oil
1 tablespoon lemon juice
1 handful mint

Put the potatoes in a saucepan of cold water with some sea salt and bring to the boil over high heat. When the water reaches boiling point, cover with a lid and remove from the heat. Leave the potatoes to sit for 30 minutes. Put the thyme, chives and sumac onto a plate and roll the tuna in the herbs until each fillet is covered.

Heat a frying pan over high heat and add the 2 tablespoons of olive oil. Sear the tuna fillets for 2 minutes on each side. Remove the pan from the heat. Allow the tuna to sit in the pan until ready to serve.

To make the dressing, mix together 4 tablespoons of the extra virgin olive oil and lemon juice in a bowl. Drain the potatoes and return them to the saucepan. Using a spoon, break up the potatoes and add the remaining extra virgin olive oil. Season well.

Slice the tuna into bite-sized pieces and serve on top of the potatoes. Scatter with the mint leaves and drizzle with dressing.

seared snapper with spiced butter lamb fillet with
cumin and tomato spiced barramundi cajun-roasted
turkey fish tagine cider-glazed pork loin spiced
tomato and prawns honeyed duck breast with chinese
cabbage chermoula kingfish quince and red wine duck
cashew curry grilled chicken with aioli thyme and
sumac-seared tuna with minted potatoes rice with
tomatoes and spinach seared lamb on ginger lentils

03 mains

chicken curry braised eggplant with water chestnuts
spiced ocean trout chilli mint lamb with saffron
vegetables baked leeks with seared salmon spiced
pork with warm greens baked salmon with hijiki and
radish salad moroccan lamb chipotle chicken spice

potato, capsicum and zucchini curry

serves 4

500 g (1 lb 2 oz) new potatoes, sliced in half
3 tablespoons olive oil
2 large red onions, halved, sliced into eighths
2 garlic cloves, crushed
1 teaspoon ground turmeric
1 tablespoon grated fresh ginger
1 teaspoon fennel seeds, lightly crushed
3 red chillies, seeded and finely chopped
400 ml (14 fl oz) coconut milk
1 red capsicum (pepper), cut into thick strips
5 makrut (kaffir lime) leaves
500 g (1 lb 2 oz) zucchini (courgettes), sliced
4 tablespoons lime juice
2 teaspoons fish sauce
3 handfuls coriander (cilantro) leaves

Put the potatoes in a saucepan and cover with cold water. Bring to the boil, cover and remove from the heat. Meanwhile, heat the olive oil in a saucepan over medium heat. Add the onions, garlic, turmeric, ginger, fennel seeds and chillies. Cook until the onions are soft, then add the coconut milk, capsicum and makrut leaves. Add the strained potatoes, cover and simmer for 15 minutes. Add the zucchini and cook for a further 5 minutes. When ready to serve, add the lime juice and fish sauce. Garnish with coriander leaves.

seared snapper with spiced butter

80 g (2³/4 oz) butter, softened
1 onion, finely diced
1 tablespoon brown mustard seeds
1 teaspoon cayenne pepper
1 teaspoon curry powder
1 small handful finely chopped
   coriander (cilantro) leaves
4 x 175 g (6 oz) snapper fillets
1 tablespoon vegetable oil
steamed green beans, lime wedges
   and mixed leaf salad, to serve

Put 20 g (³/4 oz) of butter in a frying pan over medium heat and add the diced onion. Sauté until the onion is soft and lightly golden. Add the mustard seeds, cayenne pepper and curry powder and cook for a further 2 minutes. Remove from the heat and set aside to cool. When the onion mixture has cooled, fold in the remaining butter and coriander.

Rinse the snapper fillets in cold water and pat dry with some paper towels.

Heat the oil in a frying pan over high heat and add the snapper fillets, skin side down. Fry for several minutes until the skin is lightly browned, then flip the fish over and cook the other side for a further 2–3 minutes, depending on the thickness of the fillet. Serve on a bed of green beans with the spiced butter, some lime wedges and a mixed leaf salad.

lamb fillet with cumin and tomato

serves 4

2 large ripe tomatoes, cut into eighths
1/2 tablespoon sea salt
1 teaspoon ground cumin
1 tablespoon olive oil
1 red onion, halved and cut
  into wedges
1 tablespoon oil
500 g (1 lb 2 oz) lamb backstrap or
  loin fillet, trimmed
100 g (3 1/2 oz) English spinach leaves

Preheat the oven to 180°C (350°F/ Gas 4). Put the tomatoes in a roasting dish and sprinkle them with the salt, cumin, olive oil and onion. Roast for 20 minutes.

When the tomatoes are almost ready, heat an ovenproof frying pan over high heat and add the oil. Sear the lamb backstrap or fillet on all sides until it is well browned and then put in the oven for 5–8 minutes, depending on how well done you like it. Remove the tomatoes and lamb from the oven.

Divide the spinach leaves between four plates and top with the tomato pieces. Slice the lamb against the grain into thin slices, arrange over the tomatoes, drizzle with the pan juices and season with freshly ground black pepper.

fish tagine

4 tablespoons olive oil
1 large red onion, roughly chopped
10 saffron threads
1 teaspoon ground cumin
4 large all-purpose potatoes, sliced
   into bite-sized pieces
2 celery sticks, roughly chopped
400 g (14 oz) tin chopped tomatoes
1 small cinnamon stick
600 g (1 lb 5 oz) thick snapper fillets,
   cut into 4 cm (1½ in) chunks
1 handful flat-leaf (Italian) parsley
2 tablespoons finely chopped
   preserved lemon

Heat the olive oil in a large deep frying pan or casserole pot over medium heat. Add the onion, saffron and cumin and cook until the onion is soft and slightly caramelized. Add the potatoes, celery, tomatoes, cinnamon and 250 ml (9 fl oz/1 cup) of water. Bring to the boil, then reduce the heat to a simmer and cook for 10 minutes. When the potatoes are soft, season the fish fillets with sea salt and add them to the stew. Simmer for a further 10 minutes, then season with freshly ground black pepper. Garnish with the parsley leaves and preserved lemon and serve with warm crusty bread.

spiced fish fillets   serves 4

12 whole macadamia nuts
1/4 white onion, finely diced
4 garlic cloves
2 red chillies, seeded and finely
    chopped
2 teaspoons finely grated fresh ginger
1 teaspoon ground turmeric
4 tablespoons tamarind water (basics)
1 teaspoon soy sauce
4 x 200 g (7 oz) firm white fish fillets
125 ml (4 fl oz/1/2 cup) coconut milk
steamed Asian greens, to serve

Preheat the oven to 200°C (400°F/ Gas 6). Whiz the nuts, onion, garlic, chillies, ginger, turmeric, tamarind water and soy sauce to a paste in a blender or food processor. Rinse the fish fillets in cold water and pat dry with paper towels. Rub half the paste over the fish, put it on a baking tray and bake for 12 minutes.

Put the remaining half of the paste in a small saucepan and add the coconut milk. Stir over medium heat.

Serve the fish with steamed Asian greens and the coconut sauce.

cajun-roasted turkey serves 4

1 kg (2 lb 4 oz) English spinach
1 boneless turkey breast
  (about 1.5 kg/2 lb 12 oz)
1 tablespoon olive oil
2 tablespoons sweet Cajun spice mix
20 g (3/4 oz) thyme
cranberry sauce, to serve

Preheat the oven to 180°C (350°F/ Gas 4). Blanch the spinach in boiling water and then drain. Cut into the turkey breast to make a pocket for the spinach, then rub it with the oil and spice mix. Put the breast onto a sheet of baking paper large enough to wrap around it. Squeeze any excess moisture from the spinach and stuff it into the pocket of the breast. Season with sea salt and freshly ground black pepper and cover with a sprinkling of thyme sprigs. Wrap the paper around the breast and secure with cooking twine. Put the turkey onto a baking tray and bake for 40 minutes.

Remove the turkey from the oven and reserve any of the juices. Slice the turkey, divide between warm serving plates and pour over the reserved liquid. Serve with cranberry sauce.

cashew curry

serves 4

2 onions, diced
3 garlic cloves, crushed
4 cm (1¹/₂ in) piece fresh ginger,
  chopped
1 tablespoon olive oil
1 teaspoon turmeric
1 small cinnamon stick
6 curry leaves
1 lime, juiced
3 red capsicums (peppers), cut into
  1 cm (¹/₂ in) squares
250 g (9 oz) cashew nuts
400 ml (14 fl oz) coconut milk
2 large red chillies, seeded and finely
  chopped
2 handfuls coriander (cilantro) leaves
steamed basmati rice, to serve

Put the onions, garlic and ginger into a food processor and process into a paste. Heat the olive oil in a heavy-based saucepan over medium heat and add the onion paste. Cook for 5 minutes. Add the turmeric, cinnamon, curry leaves and lime juice and cook for 2–3 minutes. Add the capsicums and cashews. Stir, then add the coconut milk and 250 ml (9 fl oz/1 cup) of water. Simmer for 1 hour. Place the curry into a large serving bowl and top with the chillies and coriander leaves. Serve with steamed basmati rice.

cider-glazed pork loin

serves 6

500 ml (17 fl oz/2 cups) apple cider
90 g (3¹/₄ oz/¹/₄ cup) honey
3 garlic cloves, peeled and finely
  chopped
3 star anise
1 cinnamon stick
1 large red chilli, split in half
2 bay leaves
1 kg (2 lb 4 oz) pork loin, skin cut off
  and reserved
3 green apples, peeled, cored and
  thickly sliced
1 tablespoon balsamic vinegar

Put the cider, honey, garlic cloves, star anise, cinnamon, chilli and bay leaves in a bowl. Cut slashes diagonally over the loin. Add the pork to the marinade. Cover and refrigerate overnight.

Heat the oven to 200°C (400°F/Gas 6). Transfer the pork to a roasting tin. Cover it with foil and roast for 40 minutes. To make the crackling, score the pork skin with a sharp knife and cut it into several strips. Put the strips in a roasting tin and brush with water. Sprinkle with salt. Roast for 20 minutes, or until the skin is golden brown. Drain off any fat.

Put the apples in a saucepan with 125 ml (4 fl oz/¹/₂ cup) of the marinating liquid. Bring to the boil and then leave to simmer for 15 minutes. Add the balsamic vinegar and season.

Uncover the pork and baste it with the pan juices. Cook for a further 20 minutes, or until the juices run clear when a skewer is inserted into the meat. Stand the pork for 10 minutes before carving. Serve with the apple relish and crackling.

honeyed duck breast with chinese cabbage

serves 4

4 duck breasts
1 teaspoon Chinese five-spice
1 teaspoon salt
40 g (1½ oz) butter
500 g (1 lb 2 oz) Chinese cabbage, finely sliced
2 tablespoons honey
2 oranges, juiced

Preheat the oven to 200°C (400°F/ Gas 6). Score the skin of the duck breasts in a crisscross pattern and rub the five-spice into the skin along with the salt.

Melt the butter in a frying pan over a medium heat, add the cabbage, then sauté for several minutes until the cabbage is soft and transparent. Season and reduce the heat to low.

Drizzle the honey over the duck breasts and roast for 15 minutes. Check that the breasts are cooked through, allow to rest for 1 minute covered with foil and then slice thinly.

Serve the duck with the cabbage and a drizzle of fresh orange juice.

chermoula kingfish   serves 4

1 tablespoon cumin seeds, roasted
1 tablespoon coriander seeds, roasted
1 tablespoon ground paprika
1 tablespoon freshly grated ginger
2 garlic cloves
1 roasted red capsicum (pepper),
   seeded and skin removed
4 tablespoons roughly chopped
   coriander (cilantro) leaves
2 tablespoons olive oil
4 x 200 g (6½ oz) kingfish fillets
   (blue-eye cod or a similar meaty
   fish can also be used)
lime wedges, to serve
mashed potato (basics), to serve

Preheat the oven to 200°C (400°F/ Gas 6). Put all the ingredients except the fish, lime wedges and mashed potato in a food processor, or use a mortar and pestle, and process to a thick paste.

Rub the paste over the fish fillets. Put the fish, skin side up, on a baking tray and season with sea salt. Bake for 12 minutes. Remove from the oven and check with the point of a small knife that the fish is cooked through. Serve with lime wedges and creamy mashed potato.

braised eggplant with water chestnuts

serves 4

4 tablespoons olive oil

2 large red chillies, seeded and finely chopped

2 garlic cloves, minced

1 tablespoon finely grated fresh ginger

4 spring onions (scallions), trimmed and cut into 2 cm (3/4 in) lengths

2 eggplants (aubergines), cut into 2 cm (3/4 in) squares

225 g (8 oz) tinned water chestnuts, drained

500 ml (17 fl oz/2 cups) vegetable stock (basics)

1 tablespoon soy sauce

1 tablespoon balsamic vinegar

150 g (5 1/2 oz) sugar snap peas

steamed white rice, to serve

Heat the olive oil in a wok or large frying pan over high heat. Add the chilli, garlic and ginger and stir-fry for 1 minute. Add the spring onions and eggplant and cook for a further 5 minutes, or until the eggplant is soft and golden brown. Add the water chestnuts, vegetable stock, soy sauce and balsamic vinegar and reduce the heat to a simmer. Simmer until the liquid is halved.

Meanwhile, blanch the sugar snap peas in boiling water until bright green. Drain and rinse under cold running water. Add the peas to the braised eggplant and cook for a further minute. Serve with white rice.

grilled chicken with aïoli

serves 4

4 chicken leg quarters
1 tablespoon finely chopped thyme
2 tablespoons ground cumin
1 teaspoon ground coriander
1 teaspoon ground paprika
1 teaspoon sea salt
1 lemon, juiced
4 tablespoons olive oil
green salad, to serve
aïoli (basics), to serve

Put the chicken pieces into a large bowl and add the thyme, cumin, coriander, paprika and sea salt. Rub the spices into the skin and then drizzle the lemon juice and olive oil over the chicken. Cover and marinate in the refrigerator for a few hours, or overnight.

Preheat the oven to 220°C (425°F/Gas 7). Heat a barbecue flat plate to medium and cook the chicken for 2–3 minutes on each side. Transfer to a baking dish and bake in the oven for 35 minutes, or until cooked through.

Serve with a green salad and a dollop of aïoli.

spiced tomato and prawns

serves 4

1 tablespoon light olive oil
1/2 teaspoon cumin seeds
2 large green chillies, seeded and
  finely chopped
1/2 teaspoon ground turmeric
250 g (9 oz) cherry tomatoes, chopped
  in half
16 large raw prawns (shrimp), peeled
  and deveined with tails intact
125 ml (4 fl oz/1/2 cup) coconut milk
1 handful Thai basil, to garnish
steamed white rice, to serve

Heat the olive oil in a frying pan over high heat and add the cumin seeds, chillies and turmeric. Reduce the heat to medium after 1 minute, add the tomatoes, and cook for a further minute. Add the prawns and cook for 2–3 minutes on each side, or until they are pink on both sides and beginning to curl up. Remove the prawns and set aside. Add the coconut milk to the pan, season with sea salt and freshly ground black pepper and simmer for 1 minute.

Meanwhile, arrange the prawns on four plates. Spoon over the coconut sauce and garnish with the Thai basil leaves. Serve with steamed white rice.

summer spiced trout serves 4

560 g (1 lb 4 oz) ocean trout fillet, skin and bones removed
1 teaspoon sesame oil
4 spring onions (scallions), trimmed and cut into 3 cm (1¼ in) lengths
185 ml (6 fl oz/¾ cup) cider vinegar
55 g (2 oz/¼ cup) sugar
2 cm (¾ in) piece fresh ginger, peeled and julienned
2 large red chillies, seeded and finely sliced
10 cm (4 in) piece young lemon grass, finely chopped
4 star anise
1 teaspoon sichuan peppercorns
udon noodles, to serve

Cut the fish into 1 cm (½ in) wide slices and put them in a single layer in a large, deep, non-metallic dish.

Put the sesame oil and the spring onions in a saucepan over medium heat and cook them until the spring onions have turned a bright green. Pour 500 ml (17 fl oz/2 cups) of water over the spring onions and mix in the vinegar, sugar, ginger, red chillies, lemon grass, star anise and peppercorns. Bring to the boil, stirring to make sure that the sugar has dissolved, and then pour the hot liquid over the ocean trout and allow to cool. Serve with udon noodles.

chicken curry

4 tablespoons olive oil
2 large red onions, finely sliced
2 garlic cloves, finely chopped
2 tablespoons grated fresh ginger
1 teaspoon ground turmeric
3 roma (plum) tomatoes, roughly
  chopped
2 red capsicums (peppers), cut into
  2 cm (3/4 in) squares
10 curry leaves
400 ml (14 fl oz) coconut milk
3 x 200 g (7 oz) skinless, boneless
  chicken breast fillets, cut into
  thick strips
3 limes, juiced
80 g (23/4 oz) coriander (cilantro) sprigs,
  roughly chopped
steamed white rice, to serve

Heat the oil in a large saucepan over medium heat and add the onions and garlic. Cook for 3 minutes, then add the ginger and turmeric. Cook for a further minute before adding the tomatoes, capsicums, curry leaves, coconut milk and chicken pieces. Simmer for 30 minutes, then season to taste. Add the lime juice and coriander and serve with steamed white rice.

seared lamb
on ginger lentils

2 tablespoons olive oil
1 red onion, finely diced
2 garlic cloves, crushed
3 tablespoons grated fresh ginger
1 teaspoon ground cumin
200 g (7 oz/1 cup) red lentils
2 lamb backstraps or pieces of fillet
  (about 500 g/1 lb 2 oz), trimmed
1 orange, zested and juiced
coriander (cilantro) leaves, roughly
  chopped, to garnish

Preheat the oven to 180°C (350°F/ Gas 4). Heat the oil in a saucepan over medium heat and tip in the diced onion and the garlic. Cook for 1–2 minutes, or until the onion starts to soften. Add the ginger, cumin and red lentils. Stir for 1–2 minutes, or until the lentils are glossy and well coated. Pour in 625 ml (21 1/2 fl oz/2 1/2 cups) of water. Simmer for 30 minutes, or until the lentils are soft.

Sear the lamb on both sides, then roast in the oven for 5 minutes. Remove the lamb, season, cover with foil and let it rest for 1 minute. Add the orange zest to the lentils with the juice. Season.

Spoon the hot lentils into 4 bowls and top with slices of lamb. Season to taste. Drizzle with the pan juices and a little extra virgin olive oil and garnish with coriander leaves.

quince and red wine duck

12 thyme sprigs
250 ml (9 fl oz/1 cup) red wine
2 garlic cloves, sliced in half
4 duck breast fillets
3 tablespoons quince paste
1 teaspoon cumin
buttered couscous (basics), to serve

Preheat the oven to 200°C (400°F/ Gas 6). Arrange the thyme sprigs over the base of a baking dish to form a bed for the duck. Add the wine and garlic to the dish. Rinse the duck fillets under cold running water and pat dry with paper towels. With a sharp knife, make several incisions through the fatty skin on each of the fillets. Rub the quince paste into the skin, sprinkle with the cumin and season with sea salt and freshly ground black pepper.

Sit the duck fillets on top of the thyme, flesh side down. Bake for 5 minutes, then remove from the oven and spread the softened quince paste over the fillets with a knife. Return to the oven for a further 10 minutes. For crispy skin, put the cooked duck under a hot grill (broiler) for 2 minutes. Allow to sit for a few minutes then slice. Serve with buttered couscous, a few thyme sprigs and a spoonful of the cooking liquid drizzled over.

chilli mint lamb with saffron vegetables serves 4

3 tablespoons olive oil

2 tablespoons harissa (basics)

80 g (2³/₄ oz) mint sprigs, leaves removed and finely chopped

1 large handful coriander (cilantro) leaves, finely chopped

4 French-trimmed lamb racks

3 onions, peeled and quartered

3 parsnips, peeled and cut into chunks

4 waxy potatoes, peeled and cut into chunks

600 g (1 lb 5 oz) pumpkin (winter squash), peeled and cut into chunks

1 teaspoon sugar

1/2 teaspoon crushed fennel seeds

20 black olives, pitted

1 teaspoon ground cumin

10 saffron threads

3 tablespoons lemon juice

Preheat the oven to 220°C (425°F/ Gas 7). Mix 2 tablespoons of the olive oil, the harissa and herbs in a bowl. Rub into the lamb. Season with sea salt and freshly ground black pepper. Put the vegetables in a baking dish and toss with the remaining olive oil, sugar, fennel seeds, olives, cumin, saffron and lemon juice. Cover with foil and bake for 30 minutes, then turn the vegetables and return uncovered to the oven. Sear the lamb in a frying pan over high heat, then put on top of the vegetables. Bake for 20 minutes. Rest the lamb for 2–3 minutes, slice and serve with the vegetables.

baked leeks
with seared salmon   serves 4

3 leeks, washed
4 spring onions (scallions), trimmed
10 saffron threads
1 tablespoon salted capers
2 tablespoons butter
1 tablespoon olive oil
4 x 150 g (5¹/₂ oz) salmon fillets
2 handfuls baby English spinach leaves

Preheat the oven to 180°C (350°F/ Gas 4). Cut the leeks and spring onions into short lengths and put them in a baking dish with the saffron, capers, butter and 185 ml (6 fl oz/ ³/₄ cup) of water. Cover with foil and bake for 1 hour.

Heat a non-stick frying pan over high heat and add the olive oil. Sear the salmon, skin side down, for 2 minutes, then turn over. Cover, reduce the heat and cook for a further 3 minutes. Divide the spinach leaves between four plates. Top with the salmon and spoon over the baked leeks.

spiced pork with warm greens

serves 4

2 tablespoons soy sauce

2 tablespoons mirin

1 tablespoon sesame oil

2 garlic cloves, crushed

1 tablespoon brown sugar

1 teaspoon Chinese five-spice

4 star anise

1 tablespoon finely grated fresh ginger

2 small pork loin fillets

1.4 kg (3 lb 2 oz/4 bunches) choy sum, washed

steamed rice, to serve

Put the soy sauce, mirin, sesame oil, garlic, brown sugar, Chinese five-spice, star anise and ginger in a large bowl. Stir until the sugar has dissolved and the ingredients are combined. Add the pork and marinate for 1 hour. Refrigerate overnight.

Preheat the oven to 180°C (350°F/Gas 4). Heat a non-stick frying pan over high heat and add the pork. Sear on both sides until golden, then transfer to a baking tray and bake for 10 minutes. Pour the remaining marinade into the frying pan with 125 ml (4 fl oz/1/2 cup) of water. Simmer for 3 minutes.

Meanwhile, steam or stir-fry the choy sum until bright green. Remove the pork from the oven and allow to rest for a few minutes.

Serve thin slices of pork with the warm greens, steamed rice and a spoonful of the sauce.

baked salmon with arame and radish salad

2 tablespoons arame or hijiki
6 umeboshi plums, seeds removed
4 tablespoons mirin
2 teaspoons sesame oil
4 x 200 g (7 oz) salmon fillets, skin on
2 tablespoons oil
300 g (10½ oz) daikon, julienned
1 tablespoon finely sliced pickled
  ginger
1 tablespoon pickled ginger juice
400 g (14 oz) watercress, leaves only

Preheat the oven to 180°C (350°F/ Gas 4). Soak the arame in warm water for 20 minutes. Mash the plums until they are soft, then add the mirin and sesame oil.

Rinse the salmon fillets in cold water and pat them dry with paper towels. Rub the plum glaze into the flesh of the fish.

Heat the oil in a frying pan with an ovenproof handle over high heat and add the salmon fillets skin side down. Sear the fish for a few minutes, then put the pan in the oven and bake the fish for 10 minutes.

Meanwhile, toss the arame, daikon, ginger and ginger juice together in a bowl with the watercress leaves. Pile the mixture onto four plates and top with the salmon fillets.

moroccan lamb   serves 4

125 ml (4 fl oz/1/2 cup) lemon juice
3 tablespoons olive oil
1 teaspoon ground cinnamon
3 garlic cloves, sliced
1 teaspoon ground cumin
finely grated zest of 1 orange
2 lamb backstraps, trimmed (about
    500 g/1 lb 2 oz)
1 handful flat-leaf (Italian) parsley
20 mint leaves, roughly chopped
20 oregano leaves
2 vine-ripened tomatoes, roughly
    chopped
buttered couscous (basics), to serve

Put the lemon juice, olive oil, cinnamon, garlic, cumin and orange zest in a glass or ceramic bowl and stir to combine. Add the lamb, cover and place in the refrigerator for 3 hours, or overnight.

Remove the lamb from the marinade and sear in a non-stick frying pan over high heat. Cook until the uncooked side is beginning to look a little bloody, then turn the lamb over. Reduce the heat and cook for a further 5 minutes. Allow to rest for a few minutes.

Toss the fresh herbs and tomato together in a bowl and divide between four plates. Slice the lamb across the grain and arrange over the tomato salad. Serve with buttered couscous.

chipotle chicken

serves 4

1 teaspoon allspice
1/2 teaspoon cinnamon
1 teaspoon ground cumin
1 teaspoon ground coriander
1 tablespoon tinned chipotle chilli,
 finely chopped
2 tablespoons oregano leaves
4 tablespoons olive oil
2 tablespoons lime juice
4 chicken drumsticks
4 chicken thighs
1 orange, zested and juiced
400 g (14 oz) tin tomatoes
2 green capsicums (peppers), cut into
 thick chunks
buttered couscous (basics), to serve
lime halves, coriander (cilantro) leaves
 and chopped green olives, to serve

Put the allspice, cinnamon, cumin, coriander, chipotle chilli, oregano, olive oil and lime juice in a large bowl and stir. Add the chicken and toss until well coated. Cover and put in the fridge to marinate for a few hours, or overnight. Heat a large frying pan over high heat. Add the chicken and cook until golden brown. Set aside on paper towels. Drain any excess fat from the pan and add the orange zest and juice, tomato, capsicum and chicken. Cover and simmer for 30 minutes. Serve on a bed of couscous with lime halves, coriander and chopped green olives.

spice-crusted fish   serves 4

2 tablespoons coriander seeds
2 tablespoons cumin seeds
1½ tablespoons sea salt
1 garlic clove
2 large handfuls flat-leaf (Italian)
  parsley
2 tablespoons extra virgin olive oil
4 x 200 g (7 oz) blue-eye cod or other
  firm white fish fillets
2 tablespoons light olive oil
mashed potato (basics), to serve
lemon wedges, to serve

Preheat the oven to 180°C (350°F/ Gas 4). Put the coriander and cumin seeds on a roasting tray and roast for 2 minutes, or until they begin to darken. Remove, cool briefly and put in a mortar and pestle or spice grinder with the salt and some freshly ground black pepper. Grind to a powder, then add the garlic, parsley and extra virgin olive oil. Work the seasoning to a paste. Rinse the cod in cold water and pat dry with paper towels. Pat the paste onto the top of each of the fish fillets, forming a thick crust that completely covers the surface.

Heat the light olive oil in a large ovenproof frying pan over high heat until it begins to shimmer. Add the fish to the pan, crust side down. Sear for 1 minute, turn over and cook for a further minute. Put the pan in the oven for 5 minutes. Remove the fish and serve on a bed of mashed potato with lemon wedges.

beef fillet with horseradish and garlic butter

1.5 kg (3 lb 5 oz) beef eye fillet
2 tablespoons freshly ground
   black pepper
3 garlic bulbs
40 g (1½ oz) butter
2 teaspoons grated fresh horseradish
   or horseradish sauce
sautéed baby carrots, to serve
sautéed chestnuts, to serve

Trim the fillet and then rub the pepper into the surface. Put on a tray and leave in the fridge, uncovered, overnight.

Preheat the oven to 200°C (400°F/ Gas 6). Put the garlic bulbs on a baking tray. Bake in the oven for 30 minutes. Remove the bulbs and allow to cool. Slice in half and squeeze out the soft garlic. Mash into the butter and mix in the horseradish. Season.

Put the fillet into a roasting tin and roast for 10 minutes. Remove the fillet and turn it over before returning it to the oven for a further 5 minutes.

Season the beef with salt, cover with foil and rest for 15 minutes. Drain any juices from the roasting tin, reserving them for later.

Return the fillet to the oven for a further 10–15 minutes, depending on how rare you like your beef. Serve in thick slices with the garlic butter, a drizzle of the pan juices and some sautéed baby carrots and chestnuts. Season with black pepper.

ginger spiced pork cutlets

serves 4

1 teaspoon smoked paprika
1 teaspoon garam masala
1/2 teaspoon ground turmeric
1 tablespoon soft brown sugar
11/2 tablespoons grated fresh ginger
2 garlic cloves, crushed
4 tablespoons olive oil
4 pork cutlets
mashed potato (basics), to serve
green salad and lemon wedges,
   to serve

Put the paprika, garam masala, turmeric, brown sugar, ginger and garlic into a bowl. Stir in the olive oil to make a thick paste. Cover the pork cutlets with the paste and allow to marinate for 30 minutes.

Heat a large non-stick frying pan over high heat and sear the pork cutlets for 3 minutes. Turn the cutlets over, reduce the heat to low and cook for a further 7–10 minutes depending on the thickness. If the cutlets are thick, cover the pan with a lid. Serve with mashed potato, green salad and a wedge of lemon.

lime and coconut fish

serves 4

2 garlic cloves
3 cm (1¹/4 in) piece galangal, peeled
   and chopped
3 small red chillies, seeded and
   chopped
3 cm (1¹/4 in) piece of ginger, peeled
   and chopped
2 lemon grass stems, trimmed and
   chopped
15 macadamia nuts
2 tablespoons olive oil
2 red onions, peeled and finely sliced
8 makrut (kaffir lime) leaves
400 ml (14 fl oz) coconut milk
2 tomatoes, diced
600 g (1 lb 5 oz) firm white fish (such
   as ling), cut into large chunks
80 g (2³/4 oz) coriander (cilantro) sprigs
steamed rice, to serve

Put the garlic, galangal, chillies, ginger, lemon grass and macadamia nuts into a food processor or blender and process until a thick paste forms.

Heat the olive oil in a frying pan over medium heat and add the onion and makrut leaves. Cook until the onions are soft.

Add the spice paste and stir until aromatic. Add the coconut milk, tomatoes and fish, then simmer for 8 minutes. Season to taste with sea salt and freshly ground black pepper. Garnish with coriander sprigs and serve with steamed rice.

spiced lentils with
lamb cutlets

serves 4

2 tablespoons olive oil
2 garlic cloves, crushed
1 red onion, finely diced
1 teaspoon finely chopped tinned
   chipotle chilli
1 teaspoon ground turmeric
95 g (3^1/$_2$ oz/^{1}/$_2$ cup) puy lentils
400 g (14 oz) tin tomatoes, roughly
   chopped
12 small French-trimmed lamb cutlets
1 handful coriander (cilantro) leaves

Put the olive oil in a saucepan over medium heat. Add the garlic, onion, chilli and turmeric and cook until the onion is soft and transparent. Add the lentils and cook for 1 minute, stirring the lentils into the onion mixture. Add the tomatoes and 500 ml (17 fl oz/ 2 cups) of water. Cover with a lid and allow to simmer for 40 minutes. When the lentils are cooked, remove from the heat and season to taste.

Heat a non-stick frying pan over high heat and sear the lamb cutlets on one side. Cook until the uncooked side begins to look a little bloody, then turn the cutlets over and cook for a further 1–2 minutes. Season with sea salt and rest for a few minutes. Spoon the lentils onto four warmed plates. Top with the cutlets and garnish with coriander leaves.

fish with a creamy
saffron sauce

12 saffron threads
1 tablespoon olive oil
6 red Asian shallots, finely diced
1 large red chilli, seeded and finely
   chopped
1 teaspoon yellow mustard seeds
1 tomato, diced
1 teaspoon soft brown sugar
4 x 180 g (6 oz) perch fillets
4 handfuls baby English spinach leaves
185 ml (6 fl oz/3/4 cup) coconut milk
lime halves and steamed white rice,
   to serve

Cover the saffron with 250 ml (9 fl oz/ 1 cup) of boiling water in a small bowl. Heat a large deep frying pan over medium heat and add the olive oil and shallots. When the shallots are soft and transparent, add the chilli, mustard seeds, tomato, sugar and saffron water. Simmer for 3 minutes before adding the fish fillets. Cover and cook for 5 minutes.

Remove the fish to four serving plates and pile the spinach leaves beside the fillets. Add the coconut milk to the sauce and simmer for 1 minute before spooning over the fish. Serve with lime and steamed white rice.

spiced duck breast   serves 4

4 duck breast fillets, skin on
2 tablespoons soft brown sugar
1/2 teaspoon sichuan peppercorns
1 star anise
1 tablespoon sea salt
125 ml (4 fl oz/1/2 cup) brandy
4 dried shiitake mushrooms
2 thin leeks, cut into 2 cm (3/4 in)
  lengths
400 g (14 oz) butternut pumpkin
  (squash), cubed
2 tablespoons light olive oil

Preheat the oven to 180°C (350°F/ Gas 4). Score the skin of the duck in a crisscross pattern. Put the brown sugar, peppercorns and star anise into a mortar and pestle with the sea salt and grind together. Rub this mixture into the duck skin. Put the brandy in a shallow dish, add the duck breasts, skin side up, cover and marinate for at least 1 hour, or overnight.

Soak the dried mushrooms in 500 ml (17 fl oz/2 cups) of boiling water for 30 minutes. Strain the liquid into a baking dish. Slice the mushrooms. Put the mushroom slices in the dish with the leeks and pumpkin and season. Cover with foil and bake for 30 minutes, or until the pumpkin is soft. Increase the oven temperature to 200°C (400°F/Gas 6).

Heat a frying pan over high heat. Sear the duck, skin side down, until lightly browned. Put the duck breasts onto a rack set over a baking tray, skin side up. Drizzle with the brandy marinade. Roast for 15 minutes. Arrange the pumpkin and leek on four plates. Top with thinly sliced duck breast.

spiced ocean trout serves 4

2 tablespoons cumin seeds
1 tablespoon coriander seeds
2 tablespoons olive oil
2 leeks, washed and finely sliced
2 carrots, peeled and finely sliced
2 celery sticks, finely sliced
250 ml (9 fl oz/1 cup) white wine
4 x 200 g (6½ oz) ocean trout fillets
1 lemon, juiced
mashed potato (basics), to serve

Put the cumin and coriander seeds in a large heavy-based frying pan over medium heat. Heat until the seeds are aromatic. Remove from the frying pan and grind in a blender, or a mortar and pestle.

Return the spices to the frying pan and add the olive oil and leeks. Cook over medium heat for 5 minutes. Add the carrot and celery and cook for a further few minutes, until both are beginning to soften. Add the white wine and 125 ml (4 fl oz/½ cup) of water and place the trout fillets over this mixture. Season with sea salt and freshly ground black pepper. Cover the pan with a lid and reduce the heat to a simmer. Cook for 6 minutes. Remove from the heat and drizzle the lemon juice over the fish fillets. Serve with mashed potato and a spoonful of the spicy sauce.

peppered beef
with pumpkin mash

serves 6

1.5 kg (3 lb 5 oz) beef eye fillet
2 tablespoons freshly ground
  black pepper
1 kg (2 lb 4 oz) pumpkin (winter
  squash)
150 g (5½ oz) butter
2 garlic cloves, crushed
30 g (1 oz) chives, finely chopped

Trim the fillet, then rub the pepper into the surface. Put on a tray and leave in the refrigerator, uncovered, overnight. Preheat the oven to 200°C (400°F/ Gas 6). Put the fillet in a roasting tray and roast for 10 minutes before turning and cooking for a further 5 minutes. Remove from the oven. Season the fillet with sea salt. Cover with foil and rest for 15 minutes. Drain any juices from the pan and reserve to pour over the meat later.

Peel the pumpkin and cut into small pieces. Put in a saucepan with salted cold water and bring to the boil. Cook until tender. Melt the butter in a small saucepan over medium heat. Add the garlic and chives, then simmer for a few minutes. When the pumpkin is cooked, drain and mash. Stir in the butter mixture and whip to a fluffy mash. Cover and set aside in a warm place. Return the fillet to the oven for a further 15 minutes. Serve in thick slices with a drizzle of pan juices and a large spoonful of mashed pumpkin.

snapper fillets with a pink peppercorn dressing

serves 4

4 tablespoons olive oil
2 tablespoons lime juice
1 teaspoon pink peppercorns
1 tablespoon finely chopped pickled
  ginger
1 handful coriander (cilantro) leaves
1 tablespoon finely chopped
  lemon grass
4 x 200 g (7 oz) snapper fillets
2 tablespoons vegetable oil
steamed green beans, sliced on the
  diagonal, to serve

To make the peppercorn dressing, put the olive oil, lime juice, peppercorns, pickled ginger, coriander and lemon grass in a bowl and stir to combine.

Rinse the snapper fillets under cold running water and pat dry with a paper towels. Season both sides of the fillets with sea salt.

Heat the vegetable oil in a frying pan over high heat and add the snapper, skin side down. Using a spatula, press the surface of the fish and cook for 1 minute, or until the skin is crispy. Turn the fillets over and reduce the heat to medium. Cook for a further 8 minutes. Spoon the pink peppercorn dressing over the snapper and serve with steamed green beans.

chicken in a smoked
chilli marinade
serves 4

1 tablespoon finely chopped
  chipotle chilli
1 teaspoon dried oregano
2 tablespoons tomato paste
  (concentrated purée)
2 tablespoons molasses or golden
  syrup
1 orange, zest removed and juiced
4 chicken leg quarters
green salad and minted yoghurt,
  to serve

Preheat the oven to 200°C (400°F/ Gas 6). Put the chilli, oregano, tomato paste, molasses, orange zest and orange juice in a large bowl and stir to combine. Add the chicken pieces and toss to coat. Cover and allow to marinate for at least 1 hour.

Place the chicken pieces on a baking tray and roast for 35–40 minutes. Insert a sharp knife into the thickest part of the chicken and ensure that the juices are clear. Serve with a green salad and minted yoghurt.

velvet pork belly with wild mushrooms

serves 4

800 g (1 lb 12 oz) pork belly
250 ml (9 fl oz/1 cup) soy sauce
500 ml (17 fl oz/2 cups) chicken stock
  (basics)
1 1/2 teaspoons Chinese five-spice
2 red chillies
1 cinnamon stick
4 star anise
1 tablespoon finely grated ginger
2 garlic cloves, crushed
2 tablespoons vegetable oil
1 tablespoon grated palm sugar
  (jaggery)
12 fresh shiitake mushrooms
100 g (3 1/2 oz) oyster mushrooms
100 g (3 1/2 oz) enoki mushrooms
steamed white rice, to serve

Preheat the oven to 180°C (350°F/ Gas 4). Put the pork belly in a saucepan and cover with water. Bring to the boil, then remove, drain and rinse. Place the soy sauce, chicken stock, half a teaspoon of Chinese five-spice, chillies, cinnamon, star anise, ginger and garlic in a baking dish. Add the pork skin side up and rub the skin with the remaining five-spice. Add enough water to cover most of the pork. Cover with foil. Bake for 4 hours. Remove the pork from the dish. Place onto a baking tray. Cover and refrigerate overnight. Reserve 375 ml (13 fl oz/ 1 1/2 cups) of the cooking liquid.

Slice the pork into 8 cm x 3 cm (3 1/4 x 1 1/4 in) wide strips. Put the reserved cooking liquid into a saucepan with the palm sugar and shiitake mushrooms. Bring to the boil. Reduce the heat and simmer for 10 minutes. Heat the oil in a large non-stick frying pan. Fry the pieces of pork belly until crisp. Add the oyster and enoki mushrooms to the saucepan just before serving. Serve with steamed white rice.

spiced cumquat chicken

1.8 kg (4 lb) whole chicken
16 fresh cumquats, halved
4 star anise
1 teaspoon sichuan peppercorns
3 tablespoons dessert wine, optional
2 tablespoons tamari or light soy sauce
mashed potato (basics) and steamed
    green beans, to serve

Preheat the oven to 200°C (400°F/ Gas 6). Rinse the chicken and pat dry with paper towels. Put the halved cumquats, star anise, peppercorns and dessert wine in a small bowl and toss to combine. Put the spiced cumquats into the cavity of the chicken. Using a skewer, secure the opening so that the cumquats remain within the chicken.

Rub the skin of the chicken with the tamari and bake in the oven for 1 hour 15 minutes, or until cooked through. Remove the chicken and check that it is cooked by pulling a leg away from the body — the juices should be clear and not pink.

Allow the chicken to rest for 10 minutes before carving. Serve with a spoonful of the baked cumquats, and mashed potatoes and steamed green beans.

cinnamon french toast rosewater fruit salad banana
and berry muffins peach waffles papaya and coconut
sambal sticky black rice hazelnut meringue with
berries cinnamon jam drops cinnamon quince with
orange mascarpone apple and blackberry cobbler berry
chocolate tart peach and blueberry shortcake rhubarb
fool chilli and vanilla syrup with fresh mango blood
plum and cinnamon jellies eccles cakes tamarind

04 sweets

ginger ice cream with red papaya ice cream trifles
with turkish delight cumin and lime cookies jaffa
mousse spiced treacle tarts frozen raspberry whip
with strawberries rhubarb syllabub spiced yoghurt
with fresh fruit rhubarb jelly bitter chocolate

cinnamon french toast

serves 5

5 thick slices white bread, crusts
  removed
1 egg
1 tablespoon sugar
1 teaspoon ground cinnamon
125 ml (4 fl oz/1/2 cup) milk
butter, for frying
extra sugar, for sprinkling
160 g (51/2 oz) plain yoghurt, to serve
fresh seasonal fruit, to serve
100 ml (31/2 fl oz) maple syrup, to serve
2 tablespoons finely chopped toasted
  pecans, to serve

Cut each slice of bread in half to make rectangles. Beat the egg, sugar and cinnamon in a bowl and then add the milk. Melt the butter in a frying pan over medium heat. Dip the bread into the sweet milk mixture, covering both sides. Sprinkle one side of each piece of bread with sugar and gently fry, sugar side down, for 3 minutes, or until golden. Sprinkle the tops with a little sugar and flip over. Cook until golden and serve with yoghurt, fruit, maple syrup and a sprinkle of pecans.

rosewater fruit salad serves 6

70 g (2¹/4 oz) dried figs
70 g (2¹/4 oz) dried apricots
70 g (2¹/4 oz) pitted prunes
55 g (2 oz/¹/4 cup) sugar
3 tablespoons orange juice
1 cinnamon stick
2 star anise
¹/2 teaspoon rosewater
250 ml (9 fl oz/1 cup) plain yoghurt,
  to serve
90 g (3¹/4 oz/1 cup) flaked toasted
  almonds, to serve

Cut the dried fruit into bite-sized pieces and place in a small bowl. Place the sugar, 250 ml (9 fl oz/1 cup) of water, the orange juice, cinnamon and star anise in a small saucepan and bring to the boil over medium heat, stirring to dissolve the sugar. Boil gently for 5–6 minutes until a light syrup forms. Remove from the heat and stir the rosewater through. Pour the liquid over the prepared dried fruit and allow to soak for several hours, or preferably overnight.
Serve with yoghurt and sprinkled with the flaked almonds.

banana and berry muffins

makes 8

250 g (9 oz/2 cups) plain (all-purpose)
  flour
2 teaspoons baking powder
1/2 teaspoon ground cinnamon
2 ripe bananas, mashed
150 g (5 1/2 oz/1 cup) fresh or frozen
  blueberries
3 tablespoons honey
3 tablespoons vegetable oil
1 large egg
185 ml (6 fl oz/3/4 cup) milk
cinnamon sugar and strawberries,
  to garnish

Preheat the oven to 180°C (350°F/ Gas 4). Sift the flour, baking powder, cinnamon and a pinch of salt into a large bowl. Add the banana and blueberries and, using a fork, lightly toss the fruit through the flour. Whisk together the honey, vegetable oil, egg and milk in a small bowl. Add the liquid ingredients to the dry ingredients and combine.

Spoon the batter into a lightly greased 8-hole muffin tin. Top with cinnamon sugar and a halved strawberry. Bake for 20 minutes. Serve immediately.

peach waffles

makes 16

waffles
250 g (9 oz/2 cups) self-raising flour
2 teaspoons ground cinnamon
170 g (6 oz/3/4 cup caster (superfine)
    sugar
75 g (21/2 oz) butter, melted
3 eggs, separated
625 ml (211/2 fl oz/21/2 cups) milk

110 g (33/4 oz/1/2 cup) sugar
1/2 vanilla bean, split and seeds
    scraped
juice of 1 lemon
2 large freestone peaches, peeled,
    stoned and cut into eighths

To make the waffles, sift the flour and cinnamon in a bowl. Add the sugar, mix well and make a well in the centre. In a jug, mix together the melted butter, egg yolks and milk and pour quickly into the flour mixture, whisking to form a smooth batter. In a seperate bowl, whisk the egg whites until soft peaks form and gently fold through the batter.

Preheat and lightly grease a waffle iron. Spoon a small amount of the mixture onto the iron, close the lid and cook the waffle until golden. Repeat with the remaining mixture.

Put 400 ml (14 fl oz) of water, the sugar, vanilla and lemon juice in a saucepan and bring to the boil, stirring to dissolve the sugar. Add the peach segments and return to the boil. Reduce the heat and simmer gently for 2 minutes. Put the fruit in a bowl and reduce the liquid over medium heat for 10–15 minutes to produce a thick syrup. Pour over the peaches. Serve a waffle segment topped with a piece of peach and drizzle with the syrup.

sticky black rice

200 g (7 oz/1 cup) black rice
80 g (2³/₄ oz/¹/₃ cup) soft brown sugar
125 ml (4 fl oz/¹/₂ cup) coconut milk
red papaya or banana, to serve

Soak the black rice in plenty of cold water for 1 hour. Drain, then rinse. Drain again and put into a saucepan with 500 ml (17 fl oz/2 cups) of water. Bring to the boil, stirring occasionally, then reduce the heat to low, cover with a lid and allow to simmer for 35 minutes. Remove the lid and stir through the brown sugar, a pinch of salt and the coconut milk. Simmer over low heat for a further 10 minutes, then remove and allow to cool. Serve spooned over sliced red papaya or banana and drizzle with coconut milk.

hazelnut meringue
with berries   serves 6

2 egg whites
115 g (4 oz/$1/2$ cup) caster (superfine)
   sugar
35 g ($11/4$ oz/$1/3$ cup) ground hazelnuts
310 ml ($103/4$ fl oz/$11/4$ cups) cream
   (whipping)
1 teaspoon natural vanilla extract
450 g (1 lb) mixed strawberries
   (quartered), raspberries and
   blackberries

Preheat the oven to 150°C (300°F/ Gas 2). Whisk the egg whites until they form soft peaks and then slowly add the sugar, continuing to beat until the mixture is stiff. Fold in the hazelnuts.

Line two baking trays with baking paper. Divide the meringue between them, putting a big dollop in the middle of each tray. Using the back of a spoon, spread the mixture out until you have two 20 cm (8 in) circles.

Bake for 40 minutes. Turn the oven off, but leave the meringues in the oven, with the door ajar, for 30 minutes.

Whip the cream and fold in the vanilla extract. When the meringues are cool, put one of the rounds on a serving plate and top with some of the cream and half the berries, arranging them so that they make a flat surface for the next meringue layer. Put the other meringue on top and decorate with the cream and remaining berries. Allow to sit for 15 minutes before serving.

cinnamon jam drops

makes 36

90 g (3¹/4 oz/³/4 cup) self-raising flour
1 teaspoon ground cinnamon
45 g (1¹/2 oz/¹/4 cup) rice flour
75 g (2¹/2 oz) unsalted butter, softened
75 g (2¹/2 oz/¹/3 cup) sugar
1 egg, beaten
500 g (1 lb 2 oz) berry jam

Preheat the oven to 180°C (350°F/ Gas 4). Sift together the flour, cinnamon and rice flour. In a bowl, cream the butter and sugar until light and fluffy, then gradually add the egg, beating well. Fold into the sifted ingredients until just combined. Roll a teaspoon of the batter into a ball and place on a baking tray lined with baking paper. Repeat with the remaining mixture. Press a deep indent into the centre of each ball and fill with a little berry jam. Bake for 8–10 minutes, or until golden.

cinnamon quince with
orange mascarpone serves 4

3 quinces
185 ml (6 fl oz/3/4 cup) red wine
125 ml (4 fl oz/1/2 cup) fresh orange
  juice
80 g (23/4 oz/1/3 cup) soft brown sugar
1 cinnamon stick
orange mascarpone (basics), to serve
gingerbread (basics), to serve

Preheat the oven to 180°C (350°F/ Gas 4). Peel and core the quinces and slice into eighths. Put in a baking dish and cover with the red wine, orange juice, brown sugar and cinnamon.

Add 250 ml (9 fl oz/1 cup) of water and cover with foil. Bake for 2 hours. Remove the foil and turn the quince pieces to coat in the liquid. Return to the oven and bake for a further 1 hour, or until the liquid has reduced to a syrup.

Divide between four plates and serve with a dollop of orange mascarpone and a drizzle of the quince syrup. For a richer wintertime dessert, serve the quince with slices of gingerbread.

apple and blackberry cobbler

serves 6

250 g (9 oz) plain (all-purpose) flour
1 tablespoon baking powder
160 g (5³/4 oz/³/4 cup) caster (superfine)
  sugar
60 g (2¹/4 oz) vegetable shortening
  (copha)
50 g (1³/4 oz) unsalted butter
1 egg
4 tablespoons milk
6 green apples, peeled, cored and cut
  into eighths
300 g (10¹/2 oz) frozen blackberries
2 tablespoons lemon juice
1 teaspoon cinnamon
whipped cream, to serve

Preheat the oven to 210°C (415°F/ Gas 6–7). Combine the flour, baking powder, 1 tablespoon of sugar and a pinch of salt in a large bowl. Cut the shortening and butter into small cubes and rub into the flour with your fingertips until the mixture resembles breadcrumbs. Whisk together the egg and milk, then stir into the flour mixture until combined. Turn out the dough onto a floured surface and knead.

Combine the apples, blackberries, 4 tablespoons of sugar, lemon juice and cinnamon and put in a deep baking dish. Break off pieces of the dough and scatter them over the top of the fruit until roughly covered. Sprinkle with the remaining sugar and bake for 40 minutes. Serve with whipped cream.

berry chocolate tart   serves 8

105 g (3¹/2 oz/¹/3 cup) strawberry jam
1 pre-baked chocolate tart case
    (basics)
160 g (5³/4 oz) unsalted butter
200 g (7 oz) dark chocolate
3 egg yolks
2 eggs
80 g (2³/4 oz/¹/3 cup) caster (superfine)
    sugar
2 tablespoons Grand Marnier
unsweetened cocoa powder,
    for dusting
fresh berries, to serve

Preheat the oven to 180°C (350°F/ Gas 4). Spoon the jam onto the base of the tart case and put in the oven for 2 minutes. Remove the tart case and use a pastry brush to brush the warm jam gently over the base until it is glazed all over.

Melt the butter and chocolate together in a saucepan over low heat. Beat the yolks, eggs and sugar until they are fluffy. Pour the melted chocolate and Grand Marnier into the eggs and continue to beat for 1 minute.

Pour the chocolate filling into the tart case and return to the oven for 5 minutes. Allow to sit for at least 2 hours before serving. Dust with cocoa powder and serve with berries.

peach and blueberry shortcake

60 g (2¼ oz/½ cup) plain (all-purpose) flour

30 g (1 oz/¼ cup) cornflour (cornstarch)

45 g (1½ oz/¼ cup) soft brown sugar

½ teaspoon ground ginger

½ teaspoon baking powder

1½ tablespoons unsalted butter, softened

1 egg yolk

150 g (5½ oz) blueberries

40 g (1½ oz) caster (superfine) sugar

2 peaches, peeled, stoned and sliced

icing (confectioner's) sugar, for dusting

whipped cream, to serve

Preheat the oven to 180°C (350°F/Gas 4). Sift the flours, sugar, ginger and baking powder into a bowl, then work in the butter and the egg yolk to form a soft dough. If the dough is too stiff, add a splash of cold water. Roll out the pastry and cut into four 8 cm (3 in) rounds.

Put the pastry on a baking tray lined with baking paper. Bake for 12 minutes, or until golden brown. Allow to cool. Heat a non-stick frying pan over medium heat and add the blueberries, 2 tablespoons of water and the caster sugar. Heat until the sugar has melted and the berries look glossy and their skins start to split. Arrange the shortbread on four plates with the peaches on top. Spoon over the berries and dust with icing sugar. Serve with whipped cream.

rhubarb fool

400 g (14 oz) rhubarb
2 tablespoons sugar
2 oranges, juiced
115 g (4 oz/1/2 cup) dark brown sugar
300 ml (101/2 fl oz) cream (whipping),
  whipped
cardamom almond bread (basics),
  to serve

Trim and rinse the rhubarb before chopping into 2 cm (3/4 in) lengths. Put the rhubarb into a saucepan over low heat with the sugar and orange juice. Cover and simmer for 15 minutes. Remove and allow to cool. Spoon a little of the rhubarb into the base of four glass serving bowls. Sprinkle with the brown sugar and top with the whipped cream. Spoon another layer of rhubarb over the cream and lightly sprinkle with more brown sugar. Serve with cardamom almond bread.

chilli and vanilla syrup with fresh mango

serves 4

220 g (7³/₄ oz/1 cup) sugar
1 vanilla bean, split lengthways
1 large red chilli, seeded and finely
  chopped
1 lime, juiced
3 mangoes, peeled and flesh cut into
  thick strips
lime sorbet (basics), to serve

Put the sugar, vanilla bean and chilli into a small saucepan with 500 ml (17 fl oz/2 cups) of water. Bring to the boil then reduce the heat and allow to simmer for 15 minutes. Allow to cool then stir in the lime juice.

Divide the mango between four chilled bowls and top with scoops of the lime sorbet. Drizzle over the chilli syrup and serve immediately.

blood plum and cinnamon jellies

serves 6

6 blood plums, quartered and stoned
230 g (8¹/₂ oz/1 cup) caster (superfine) sugar
1 cinnamon stick
1 vanilla bean, split in half lengthways
1–2 oranges, juiced
6 gelatine sheets
cream (whipping), to serve

Put the plums, sugar, cinnamon stick, vanilla bean and 750 ml (26 fl oz/ 3 cups) of water into a saucepan. Bring to the boil, then reduce the heat. Continue to simmer for 30 minutes. Remove from the heat and strain the plum syrup through a fine sieve or muslin. Pour the syrup into a measuring jug and add enough orange juice to make 600 ml (21 fl oz) of plum syrup.

Soak the gelatine sheets in a large bowl of cold water for 10–15 minutes, or until very soft. Return the syrup to the saucepan and heat over low heat until the syrup is warm. Squeeze any excess liquid from the gelatine and add to the warm syrup.

Pour the jelly into six 100 ml (3¹/₂ fl oz) moulds and put in the refrigerator for 3 hours, or until set. Serve with a drizzle of cream.

citrus syrup cake   serves 10

250 g (9 oz) unsalted butter
250 g (9 oz) caster (superfine) sugar
4 eggs
100 g (3^1/$_2$ oz) plain yoghurt
2 lemons, zested and juiced
2 oranges, zested and juiced
2 limes, zested and juiced
250 g (9 oz/2 cups) self-raising flour
220 g (7^3/$_4$ oz/1 cup) sugar
cream (whipping), to serve

Preheat the oven to 180°C (350°F/ Gas 4). Grease and line a 24 cm (9^1/$_2$ in) spring-form cake tin with baking paper. Cream the butter and sugar, then fold in the eggs, yoghurt and citrus zest. Sift in the flour and fold it through the batter. Spoon the batter into the prepared cake tin. Bake for 45 minutes, or until the cake is golden brown and a skewer inserted into the centre comes out clean.

Meanwhile, put the citrus juice in a saucepan and add the sugar. Bring to the boil and stir until the sugar has dissolved. Remove from the heat.

When the cake is cooked, remove from the oven and prick the top of the cake all over with a skewer. Pour over half the syrup, reserving the rest for serving later. Allow to cool. Serve with reserved syrup and whipped cream.

tamarind ginger ice cream with red papaya

4 egg yolks

145 g (5 oz/$^2/_3$ cup) caster (superfine) sugar

250 ml (9 fl oz/1 cup) milk

100 g (3$^1/_2$ oz/$^1/_3$ cup) tamarind purée

300 ml (10$^1/_2$ fl oz) cream (whipping)

110 g (3$^3/_4$ oz/$^1/_2$ cup) finely sliced ginger in syrup

2 small ripe red papayas, halved, seeded and peeled

Whisk the yolks and the sugar together in a bowl until they double in volume. Bring the milk to the boil in a saucepan and, when it begins to froth on the surface, pour it into the yolk mixture. Whisk together before returning to the saucepan and placing over low heat. Stir until the mixture has thickened and coats the back of a wooden spoon. Remove from the heat and strain into a chilled bowl. Stir in the tamarind purée, cream and ginger. Allow to cool. Pour the mixture into an ice cream machine. Churn according to the manufacturer's instructions.

If you don't have an ice cream machine, pour the mixture into a small metal bowl and place in the freezer. Take the ice cream mixture out of the freezer every couple of hours and beat. This will break up any ice crystals as they form. Serve the ice cream scooped into a red papaya half.

ice cream trifles
with turkish delight serves 6

250 g (9 oz) raspberries or strawberries
6 cubes Turkish delight
12 plain chocolate biscuits (cookies)
500 g (1 lb 2 oz oz/2 cups) vanilla ice
  cream (basics), scooped
80 g (2³/4 oz/¹/2 cup) blanched
  almonds, toasted

Purée the berries to form a sauce and set aside. Cut the Turkish delight into eighths so as to make small cubes. Break the biscuits into small pieces and set aside.

Layer the ice cream, biscuits, Turkish delight and blanched almonds into six chilled glasses and top with the berry sauce. Serve immediately.

cumin and lime cookies

120 g (4¹/₄ oz) unsalted butter

150 g (5¹/₂ oz/²/₃ cup) caster (superfine) sugar

1 teaspoon ground cumin

1 teaspoon natural vanilla extract

2 tablespoons of lime juice, plus the grated zest of 1 lime

1 egg

150 g (5¹/₂ oz/1¹/₄ cups) plain (all-purpose) flour

1 teaspoon baking powder

whipped cream and fresh fruit, to serve

Preheat the oven to 180°C (350°F/ Gas 4). Cream the butter and sugar then fold in the cumin, vanilla, lime juice, lime zest and egg. Sift in the flour and baking powder and stir together. Spoon the batter onto a baking sheet lined with baking paper – use 1 heaped tablespoon of mixture per cookie. Bake for 12 minutes, or until golden brown and allow to cool on a wire rack.

Serve with whipped cream and slices of ripe fruit such as figs, nectarines and peaches.

jaffa mousse

140 g (5 oz) bitter chocolate
4 tablespoons Grand Marnier
4 egg yolks
40 g (1 1/2 oz/1/3 cup) unsweetened
  cocoa powder
2 teaspoons grated orange zest
185 ml (6 fl oz/3/4 cup) cream
  (whipping), whipped
4 oranges

Melt the chocolate and 2 tablespoons of Grand Marnier in a bowl set over a saucepan of simmering water. Add the egg yolks, one at a time, stirring each one well into the chocolate mixture before adding the next. The chocolate may begin to stiffen but it will soon become smooth again. When you have added all the yolks, remove the chocolate mixture from the heat and allow to cool slightly.

Fold the cocoa and grated orange zest into the whipped cream, then fold the cream into the chocolate. Pour the mixture into a bowl and leave it in the refrigerator for several hours to chill.

Peel the oranges with a sharp knife and cut into slices. Put the orange slices in a bowl with 2 tablespoons of Grand Marnier. Divide the oranges between dessert plates and top with a spoonful of the mousse.

spiced treacle tarts makes 24

45 g (1 1/2 oz/1/2 cup) desiccated
   coconut
125 ml (4 fl oz/1/2 cup) golden or maple
   syrup
1/4 teaspoon ground cardamom
1 tablespoon lime juice
2 teaspoons finely chopped lime zest
1 egg yolk, beaten
24 pre-baked sweet tartlet cases
   (basics)
icing (confectioners') sugar, for dusting

Preheat the oven to 180°C (350°F/ Gas 4). Put all the ingredients except the tart shells and icing sugar in a bowl and mix. Spoon a heaped teaspoon of the filling into each of the pastry cases and bake for 10 minutes. Remove and cool on a wire rack. Dust with icing sugar before serving.

frozen raspberry whip with strawberries

serves 4-6

150 g (5¹/2 oz) raspberries
1 teaspoon lemon juice
115 g (4 oz/¹/2 cup) caster (superfine) sugar
1 egg white
500 g (1 lb 2 oz) strawberries
1 tablespoon icing (confectioners') sugar

Whip the raspberries, lemon juice, sugar and egg white with electric beaters for 10 minutes, or until the mixture is light and fluffy and has tripled in size. Spoon into a container and put into the freezer for several hours, or overnight, until frozen.

Just prior to serving, hull and halve the strawberries, reserving some whole ones. Sprinkle the strawberry halves with the icing sugar and lightly toss until well coated. Set aside for 5 minutes before serving with a scoop of the frozen raspberry whip. Garnish with the whole strawberries.

rhubarb syllabub

**500 g (1 lb 2 oz) rhubarb, cut into
small pieces**
**90 g (3¹/₄ oz/¹/₃ cup) caster (superfine)
sugar**
**250 ml (9 fl oz/1 cup) thick
(double/heavy) cream**
16 macaroons or amaretti
4 tablespoons Madeira
1 teaspoon finely grated lemon zest
¹/₄ teaspoon almond extract

Put the rhubarb in a saucepan with the sugar, then cover and cook over medium heat until the rhubarb is soft, stirring occasionally to prevent it from sticking. Allow to cool.

Whip the cream. Refrigerate and cover until needed.

Crumble two macaroons into each of eight glasses. Fold the Madeira, lemon zest and almond extract into the rhubarb before lightly folding the rhubarb through the whipped cream. Spoon the rhubarb cream over the macaroons and serve.

spiced yoghurt
with fresh fruit   serves 6

2 cinnamon sticks
2 star anise
2 cloves
2 vanilla beans, split lengthways
2 cardamom pods, split
250 ml (9 fl oz/1 cup) cream (whipping)
1 tablespoon sugar
300 g (10¹/₂ oz) Greek-style yoghurt
fresh fruit, to serve

Put the cinnamon, star anise, cloves, vanilla beans, cardamom pods and cream in a small saucepan over low heat. Allow to simmer for 30 minutes. Remove from the heat, strain, then stir in the sugar before allowing to cool. Fold the spiced cream through the yoghurt and serve drizzled over fruit.

rhubarb jelly

serves 8

1 kg (2 lb 4 oz) rhubarb
350 g (12 oz/1½ cups) caster (superfine) sugar
grated zest and juice of 1 orange
1 teaspoon ground cinnamon
300 ml (10½ fl oz) orange juice
8 gelatine sheets
vanilla ice cream (basics), to serve

Preheat the oven to 180°C (350°F/ Gas 4). Chop the rhubarb into 3 cm (1¼ in) lengths and put in a ovenproof glass or ceramic dish. Add the sugar, orange zest and juice, cinnamon and 500 ml (17 fl oz/2 cups) of water. Cover with foil. Bake for 1 hour. Strain the rhubarb through a sieve into a jug. Add enough orange juice to make up to 900 ml (31 fl oz) of liquid.

Soak the gelatine leaves in a bowl of cold water until softened. Lightly oil a jelly mould or glass bowl with vegetable oil, then set aside.

Put 250 ml (9 fl oz/1 cup) of the rhubarb liquid into a saucepan. Bring almost to the boil. Remove from the heat. Squeeze the softened gelatine sheets to remove any excess water and add them to the hot liquid. Swirl until dissolved, then add the liquid to the remaining rhubarb juice. Stir to combine. Pour the jelly into the mould. Refrigerate for 5 hours to chill and set. To turn out, warm the outside of the mould with a cloth rinsed in hot water, cover with a plate, then turn it over. Serve with vanilla ice cream.

bitter chocolate tartlets

150 g (5^1/$_2$ oz) unsalted butter
200 g (7 oz) dark chocolate
3 egg yolks
2 eggs
60 g (2^1/$_4$ oz/^{1}/$_4$ cup) caster (superfine)
  sugar
2 tablespoons Tia Maria
6 pre baked mini shortcrust tart cases
  (basics)
unsweetened cocoa powder,
  for dusting
whippped cream, to serve

Preheat the oven to 180°C (350°F/ Gas 4). Melt the butter and chocolate together in a saucepan over very low heat. Beat the egg yolks, eggs and sugar until they are light and fluffy. Pour the melted chocolate and Tia Maria into the egg mixture and continue to beat for 1 minute. Pour the chocolate filling into the tart cases and bake for 5 minutes.

Remove from the oven and allow to sit for 1 hour before serving. Dust with cocoa powder and serve with whipped cream.

coffee granita

115 g (4 oz/1/2 cup) sugar
1 teaspoon finely grated lemon zest
1 tablespoon lemon juice
500 ml (17 fl oz/2 cups) strong
   espresso coffee

Put the sugar and 125 ml (4 fl oz/ 1/2 cup) water in a saucepan over high heat. Stir until the sugar has dissolved. Remove from the heat and stir in the lemon zest, lemon juice and coffee. Allow to cool, then cover and put in the refrigerator. Pour the chilled mixture into a cake tin or large shallow metal container. (The mixture must freeze quickly and a shallow metal container chills the liquid faster.) Cover and put in the freezer. After 1 hour, use a fork to drag the icy crystals from the edges of the container into the centre. Return to the freezer and repeat this process every 30 minutes until the mixture is completely frozen and icy. If making in advance, remove from the freezer 1 hour before serving, thaw slightly, then break up the crystals again and return to the freezer for a further 30 minutes before serving.

blackberry fool

300 g (10¹/₂ oz/2¹/₂ cups) blackberries
60 g (2¹/₄ oz/¹/₄ cup) caster (superfine)
  sugar
2 tablespoons crème de framboise
  (optional)
1 teaspoon orange flower water
325 ml (11 fl oz) cream (whipping),
  whipped
almond bread or biscotti, to serve

Put the blackberries, sugar, liqueur and orange flower water into a blender or food processor and blend to a purée.

Fold the puréed berries into the cream and spoon the mixture into four chilled glasses or small bowls. Serve with almond bread or biscotti.

ginger hearts

250 g (9 oz/2 cups) plain (all-purpose)
  flour
1 teaspoon baking powder
3 teaspoons ground ginger
1 teaspoon ground cinnamon
pinch ground cloves
85 g (3 oz) unsalted butter, softened
115 g (4 oz/1/2 cup) dark brown sugar
1 egg
1 tablespoon molasses
55 g (2 oz/1/4 cup) raw sugar

Preheat the oven to 180°C (350°F/ Gas 4). Sift the flour and spices into a bowl. In another bowl, cream the butter and brown sugar until light and fluffy, and add the egg, beating well. Stir through the molasses. Fold through the sifted dry ingredients until combined. Gather into a ball.

Roll out the dough between two sheets of baking paper to a thickness of 5 mm (1/4 in). Cut heart shapes from the dough with a 5 cm (2 in) cookie cutter and sprinkle with raw sugar. Transfer to a baking tray and bake for 12 minutes. Cool on a wire rack.

berry granita

175 g (6 oz/^{3}/$_4$ cup) caster (superfine)
  sugar
625 ml (21 fl oz/2^1/$_2$ cups) Earl Grey tea
250 g (9 oz/1^2/$_3$ cups) strawberries
juice of 1 orange
150 g (5^1/$_2$ oz/1^1/$_4$ cups) raspberries,
  to serve

Dissolve the sugar in the hot tea and set aside to cool. In a blender or food processor, blend the strawberries with the orange juice to a purée. Stir the puréed strawberries into the cool tea and pour into a plastic container about 15 x 20 cm (6 x 8 in). Cover and put in the freezer for 2 hours.

Remove from the freezer and use a fork to break up the ice crystals, mixing them back into the chilled liquid. Repeat this process every 40 minutes until you have a container filled with flavoured crushed ice. If freezing overnight, remove from the freezer and allow it to soften for 30 minutes before breaking up the crystals and returning to the freezer. To serve, layer the granita with the raspberries in tall glasses.

baked quinces with orange and cardamom almond bread

serves 4

2 large quinces, peeled, cored and
  quartered
2 oranges, juiced
60 g (2$^{1}/_{4}$ oz/$^{1}/_{4}$ cup) sugar
2 tablespoons honey
cardamom almond bread (basics)
icing (confectioners') sugar, for dusting
plain yoghurt or thick (double/heavy)
  cream, to serve

Preheat the oven to 180°C (350°F/ Gas 4). Line a baking tray with baking paper and lay the quince quarters on it. Cover them with the orange juice, sugar and honey and another piece of baking paper and put in the oven.

After an hour, reduce the oven to 140°C (275°F/Gas 1) and bake the quinces for a further 2 hours, or until they are soft and have turned a deep ruby red.

Serve the quinces with the almond bread dusted with icing sugar, and with yoghurt or thick cream.

sticky date pudding   serves 4

150 g (5¹/2 oz/scant 1 cup) pitted and
  finely chopped dates
1¹/2 teaspoons bicarbonate of soda
50 g (1³/4 oz) unsalted butter
125 g (4¹/2 oz/²/3 cup) soft brown sugar
2 eggs
1 teaspoon natural vanilla extract
1 tablespoon finely chopped glacé
  ginger
125 g (4¹/2 oz/1 cup) sifted self-raising
  flour
butterscotch sauce and whipped
  cream, to serve

Preheat the oven to 180°C (350°F/ Gas 4). Lightly grease four 300 ml (10¹/2 fl oz) ramekins. Put the dates in a bowl with the bicarbonate of soda. Pour over 150 ml (5 fl oz) boiling water and set aside for 10 minutes. Beat the butter with the brown sugar in a bowl until pale and creamy. Whisk in the eggs. Stir in the vanilla extract and add the glacé ginger. Add the self-raising flour and lightly fold it through the batter. Fold the date mixture through. Spoon the batter into the ramekins and put the ramekins onto a baking tray. Bake for 20–25 minutes, or until firm. Serve with butterscotch sauce and whipped cream.

rose-tinged rice pudding

serves 6

500 ml (17 fl oz/2 cups) milk
55 g (2 oz/1/4 cup) granulated sugar
2 teaspoons finely grated orange zest
75 g (21/2 oz/1/3 cup) short-grain rice
125 ml (4 fl oz/1/2 cup) cream
  (whipping), whipped
1 teaspoon rosewater
150 g (51/2 oz) raspberries
65 g (21/4 oz/1/2 cup) raw pistachio
  kernels, chopped

Bring the milk to the boil in a saucepan with the sugar, orange zest and a pinch of salt. Add the rice, reduce the heat and simmer for 30 minutes, stirring occasionally. When the rice has cooked, allow it to cool before folding in the whipped cream and rosewater.

Spoon the rice pudding into serving bowls and top with the raspberries and pistachios.

nectarine salad

8 nectarines, stoned, sliced into
  eighths
150 g (5^1/$_2$ oz) raspberries
1 tablespoon grated fresh ginger
45 g (1^1/$_2$ oz/^{1}/$_4$ cup) soft brown sugar
1 lime, juiced
plain yoghurt, to serve

Put all the ingredients in a large bowl
and gently toss together. Allow the
salad to marinate for 1 hour. Serve
with plain yoghurt.

chocolate parfait   serves 6

125 g (4¹/2 oz/heaped ¹/2 cup) sugar
125 g (4¹/2 oz) dark chocolate, broken
  into pieces
4 egg yolks
300 ml (10¹/2 fl oz) cream, whipped
1 tablespoon Frangelico
50 g (1³/4 oz/¹/2 cup) toasted flaked
  almonds
fresh berries and raspberry syrup
  (basics), to serve

Line a terrine or loaf tin with baking paper and set aside. Put the sugar and 150 ml (5 fl oz) water in a saucepan and bring to the boil, stirring until the sugar has dissolved. Boil for 3 minutes. Remove from the heat and add the chocolate, stirring until the chocolate has melted and the syrup is smooth.

Whisk the egg yolks in a bowl until they are pale. Slowly pour in the sugar syrup and continue to whisk until the mixture has cooled. Fold in the whipped cream, Frangelico and almonds and pour the mixture into a terrine mould. Cover and put in the freezer overnight.

To serve, turn out the parfait from the terrine or tin and with a warm knife cut into 6 thick slices. Serve with fresh berries and raspberry syrup.

baked figs with pistachios

serves 4

4 large figs
1 tablespoon soft brown sugar
1 orange, zested and juiced
20 g (3/4 oz) unsalted butter
50 g (13/4 oz/1/3 cup) pistachio nuts
1/2 teaspoon ground cinnamon
1 tablespoon honey
250 g (9 oz/1 cup) mascarpone cheese

Preheat the oven to 180°C (350°F/ Gas 4). Slice the figs into quarters lengthways from the top downwards, being careful not to slice all the way through. Sit them in a baking dish and put a heaped teaspoon of brown sugar and some of the orange zest into the centre of each fig. Divide the butter between the figs and dot it on top of the sugar. Add the pistachios and orange juice to the dish and sprinkle with a little cinnamon. Bake the figs for 10 minutes.

Meanwhile, blend the honey into the mascarpone until smooth.

To serve, carefully remove the figs from the dish and put a spoonful of honeyed mascarpone in the middle of each. Spoon over the juice and pistachios and serve while still warm.

quince and rosewater tarts

makes 12

90 g (3¹/₄ oz) quince paste
4 tablespoons orange juice
120 g (4¹/₄ oz) mascarpone cheese
¹/₂ teaspoon rosewater
2 teaspoons icing (confectioners')
  sugar
1 tablespoon ground almonds,
  lightly toasted
12 pre-baked sweet tartlet cases
  (basics)

Melt the quince paste with the orange juice in a bowl over a saucepan of simmering water. Stir well to combine, then remove and allow to cool.

Blend the mascarpone with the rosewater, icing sugar and almond meal. Spoon the mascarpone mixture into the tart shells and top with the cooled quince paste.

marinated raspberries
with coconut ice

serves 4

3 tablespoons orange juice
1 tablespoon Grand Marnier (optional)
400 g (14 oz) raspberries
3 tablespoons milk
110 g (3³/4 oz/¹/2 cup) sugar
60 g (2¹/4 oz/¹/2 cup) icing
  (confectioners') sugar
45 g (1¹/2 oz/¹/2 cup) desiccated
  coconut
10 g (¹/4 oz) butter
¹/2 teaspoon orange flower water
2 drops pink food colouring (cochineal)

Combine the orange juice and Grand Marnier in a small bowl, very gently stir in the raspberries and leave for 30 minutes to marinate.

Bring the milk and sugars to the boil and boil gently for 3 minutes. Add the coconut and butter and boil for 1 minute, then add the orange flower water and pink food colouring. Take off the heat and stir until the mixture resembles breadcrumbs. Store in an airtight container until ready to use. Pile the raspberries into glasses or bowls. Sprinkle with the coconut ice.

winter fruit crumble serves 6

300 g (10¹/2 oz) rhubarb, roughly
   chopped
1 orange, juiced
6 dried figs, finely sliced
2 green apples, peeled, cored and
   roughly chopped
60 g (2¹/4 oz/¹/4 cup) caster (superfine)
   sugar
60 g (2¹/4 oz/¹/2 cup) plain (all-purpose)
   flour
95 g (3¹/4 oz/¹/2 cup) soft brown sugar
95 g (3¹/4 oz/¹/2 cup) ground almonds
60 g (2¹/4 oz) unsalted butter
cream (whipping), to serve

Preheat the oven to 180°C (350°F/ Gas 4). Toss the rhubarb with the orange juice, figs, green apples and caster sugar and tip the mixture into an ovenproof dish.

Put the flour, brown sugar and ground almonds in a bowl, and then add the butter and rub it into the dry ingredients until the mixture begins to resemble breadcrumbs. Cover the fruit with this mixture and bake for 45 minutes. Serve with cream.

honey-spiced figs

serves 4

8 figs
juice and zest of 1 orange
12 small mint leaves, torn
1 tablespoon honey
200 ml (7 fl oz) thick (double/heavy)
  cream
1/2 teaspoon caster (superfine) sugar
1 tablespoon ground walnuts

Slice the figs, then place, overlapping, on a serving plate. Pour over the orange juice, then scatter with the orange zest and mint leaves and drizzle with the honey. Set aside. Put the cream, sugar and walnuts into a small bowl, and stir to combine. Serve the cream with the figs.

pears baked in marsala

6 ripe corella pears
50 g (1³/4 oz) butter, softened
100 g (3¹/2 oz) soft brown sugar
1 lemon, zest removed and juiced
150 ml (5 fl oz) Marsala
2 cinnamon sticks, roughly broken
thick (double/heavy) cream, to serve

Preheat the oven to 180°C (350°F/ Gas 4). With a small knife, remove the core from each of the pears. Cut a thin slice from the base of each of the pears to allow them to sit easily. Spread the butter over the skin of the pear and stand them in a baking dish. In a small bowl combine the sugar, lemon juice and marsala. Pour around the pears then add the cinnamon sticks and lemon zest.

Cover with foil and bake in the oven for 30 minutes then lower the heat to 150°C (300°F/Gas 2) and bake for a further 30 minutes. Serve with cream and spoonfuls of the baking juices.

pine nut meringues with marinated raspberries makes 6

3 egg whites
230 g (8¹/2 oz/1 cup) caster (superfine)
  sugar
100 g (3¹/2 oz) pine nuts
500 g (1 lb 2 oz) raspberries
1 teaspoon icing (confectioners') sugar
1 tablespoon Grand Marnier
300 ml (10¹/2 fl oz) thick (double/heavy)
  cream

Preheat the oven to 140°C (275°F/ Gas 1). Line a large baking tray with baking paper.

Beat the egg whites to form stiff peaks, then gradually whisk in the sugar a spoonful at a time. Continue to whisk until stiff and glossy.

Fold the pine nuts into the meringue. Spoon the mixture onto the prepared baking tray so as to form 6 mounds of meringue. Bake for 1 hour, then turn off the oven and allow the meringues to cool in the oven. Place the raspberries in a bowl and sprinkle with the icing sugar and Grand Marnier. Allow to sit for 5 minutes then lightly toss so that the liquid coats all the raspberries. Serve the meringues with a spoonful of berries and a dollop of cream.

middle-eastern summer fruit compote with honeyed yoghurt

serves 4

1 cinnamon stick

2 star anise

110 g (3³/₄ oz/¹/₂ cup) sugar

2 peaches, stoned and cut into
quarters

2 nectarines, stoned and cut into
quarters

2 apricots, stoned and cut into
quarters

2 plums, stoned and cut into quarters

1 teaspoon rosewater

150 g (5¹/₂ oz) raspberries

plain yoghurt and honey, to serve

sugared rose petals, to garnish

Put the cinnamon stick, star anise, sugar and 500 ml (17 fl oz/2 cups) of water into a saucepan and bring to the boil. Stir to ensure that the sugar has dissolved and then add the fruit pieces. Bring to the boil, then remove the fruit with a slotted spoon and place into a serving bowl. Reduce the heat and allow the syrup to simmer for a further few minutes, then add the rosewater. Spoon the syrup over the fruit and chill until ready to serve.

Serve with plain yoghurt drizzled with honey and garnish with sugared rose petals.

brandied oranges with mascarpone

serves 6

220 g (7³/4 oz/1 cup) sugar
3 cardamom pods
2 star anise
1 cinnamon stick
6 oranges
2 tablespoons brandy
250 g (9 oz) mascarpone cheese

Put the sugar, cardamom pods and cinnamon stick in a heavy-based saucepan with 170 ml (5¹/2 fl oz/ ²/3 cup) of water. Heat over medium heat, stirring occasionally, until the sugar dissolves. Boil without stirring until the syrup begins to colour. Continue to cook until the syrup turns a golden caramel colour. Remove the pan from the heat and carefully add 125 ml (4 fl oz/¹/2 cup) of warm water. Peel the oranges, removing the pith, then slice crossways into thick slices. Reassemble them and place into a deep ceramic or glass dish. Cover with the spiced syrup and brandy. Cover and chill until ready to serve. Serve the oranges with a drizzle of sauce and a spoonful of mascarpone.

fig and honey smoothie berry smoothie rhubarb smoothie chilled knight pimm's with ginger syrup berry ice greyhound negroni smooth sambucca classic rusty nail orange and rosewater ice cubes manhattan long island iced tea peach tree hot toddy mai tai mandarin ice with pomegranate hangover cure fig and honey smoothie berry smoothie rhubarb smoothie chilled knight pimm's with ginger syrup berry ice

05 drinks

greyhound negroni smooth sambucca classic rusty nail orange juice with rosewater ice cubes manhattan long island iced tea peach tree hot toddy mai tai mandarin ice with pomegranate hangover cure fig and honey smoothie berry smoothie rhubarb smoothie

fig and honey smoothie

serves 2

2 ripe black figs, roughly chopped
1 tablespoon honey
185 ml (6 fl oz/3/4 cup) plain yoghurt
8 ice cubes
3 tablespoons finely chopped walnuts

In a blender, place the figs, honey, yoghurt and ice cubes. Blend until smooth. Pour into glasses and lightly stir through walnuts.

berry smoothie

75 g (2¹/2 oz/¹/2 cup) strawberries
65 g (2¹/4 oz/¹/2 cup blackberries
60 g (2¹/4 oz/¹/2 cup) raspberries
60 ml (2 fl oz/¹/4 cup) sugar syrup
60 g (2¹/4 oz/¹/4 cup) plain yoghurt
6 ice cubes

In a blender, place the strawberries, blackberries and raspberries, sugar syrup, yoghurt and ice cubes. Blend until smooth. Pour into chilled glasses and serve immediately.

rhubarb smoothie

serves 4

stewed rhubarb
300 g (10 1/2 oz) rhubarb
55 g (2 oz/1/4 cup) caster (superfine)
  sugar

375 g (13 oz/1 1/2 cups) plain yoghurt
1/2 teaspoon ground cinnamon
16 ice cubes

Trim the rhubarb stems and cut them into 4 pieces. Place the rhubarb, sugar and 60 ml (2 fl oz/1/4 cup) of water in a stainless steel saucepan over medium heat. Cover and simmer for 10 minutes. Remove from heat and allow to cool.

In a blender, combine 250 ml (9 fl oz/ 1 cup) of cooled stewed rhubarb, yoghurt, cinnamon and ice cubes. Blend until smooth. Pour the mixture into chilled glasses and serve.

chilled knight

500 ml (17 fl oz/2 cups) Vermouth
  Rosso
1 tablespoon Fernet-Branca
60 g (2¼ oz/½ cup) seedless raisins
zest of 2 oranges
5 cardamom pods, crushed
6 cloves
1 tablespoon grated fresh ginger
2 cinnamon sticks
300 g (10½ oz/1⅓ cups) sugar
1.5 litres (52 fl oz/6 cups) red wine,
  chilled
100 ml (3½ fl oz) dark rum
300 g (10 oz) blanched almonds,
  toasted

Place the Vermouth, Fernet-Branca, raisins, orange zest, cardamom, cloves, ginger, cinnamon sticks and sugar in a saucepan and bring to the boil over medium heat. Reduce the heat to low and simmer for 10 minutes. Remove and allow to cool. Add the chilled wine, dark rum and toasted almonds, and pour into a punch bowl or large jug.

Note – Chilled knight may be served cold as a spicy late-night summer's drink, or warmed as a mulled wine on a winter's night.

pimm's with ginger syrup

serves 1

ginger syrup
75 g (2¹/₂ oz/¹/₂ cup) grated ginger
220 g (7³/₄ oz/1 cup) sugar

125 ml (4 fl oz/¹/₂ cup) fresh pineapple juice
60 ml (2 fl oz/¹/₄ cup) Pimm's
4–5 ice cubes
60 ml (2 fl oz/¹/₄ cup) soda water
lime and fresh pineapple, to garnish

To make the ginger syrup, place the ginger, sugar and 125 ml (4 fl oz/ ¹/₂ cup) of water in a small saucepan and bring to the boil. Reduce the heat and simmer for 5 minutes. Strain into a container, cool and store in the refrigerator until ready to use.

Place the pineapple juice, Pimm's, and 1¹/₂ tablespoons ginger syrup into a tall glass with ice. Top with soda water and garnish with lime and pineapple.

berry ice

sugar syrup
220 g (7³/4 oz/1 cup) sugar
250 ml (9 fl oz/1 cup) water

6 strawberries
65 g (2¹/4 oz/¹/2 cup) frozen blackberries
60 ml (2 fl oz/¹/4 cup) vodka
10 ice cubes

To make the sugar syrup, place sugar and water in a small saucepan and bring to the boil, stirring until the sugar dissolves. Cool, then store in a bottle in the refrigerator until ready to use.

Place the strawberries, blackberries, 60 ml (2 fl oz/¹/4 cup) sugar syrup, vodka and ice in a blender and blend to form an icy slush. Pour into cocktail glasses and serve immediately.

greyhound

60 ml (2 fl oz/1/4 cup) vodka
100 ml (31/2 fl oz) freshly squeezed
  grapefruit juice
a dash of Cointreau or Triple Sec
ice, to serve

Place vodka, grapefruit juice and a dash of Cointreau or Triple Sec into a tall glass. Stir, then top with ice. This drink is also suitable to serve in a large jug. Increase the quantity accordingly.

negroni

ice, to serve
30 ml (1 fl oz) Campari
30 ml (1 fl oz) sweet vermouth
30 ml (1 fl oz) gin
orange peel, to garnish

Fill two chilled glasses with ice and add Campari, sweet vermouth and gin. Lightly stir the mixture to 'marble' the different coloured alcohols, and garnish with slices of orange peel.

smooth sambucca

serves 1

30 ml (1 fl oz) crème de cacao
30 ml (1 fl oz) Sambucca

Pour the crème de cacao into a shot glass. Add the Sambucca, pouring it over the back of a spoon so that the liqueurs form two distinct layers.

classic rusty nail   serves 1

30 ml (1 fl oz) whisky
30 ml (1 fl oz) Drambuie
3 ice cubes

Place whisky, Drambuie and the ice cubes into a chilled glass. Stir well to combine. The rusty nail is the perfect drink for a late winter's night, and can be served with or without ice.

orange juice with rosewater ice cubes

serves 6

4 red organic roses, petals removed
220 g (7³/4 oz/1 cup) sugar
1 tablespoon rosewater

Put the rose petals, sugar and 310 ml (10³/4 fl oz/1¹/4 cups) of water in a large saucepan and bring to the boil. Reduce the heat and simmer for 8 minutes, or until a light syrup has been made. Remove any scum as it forms. Cool and stir in the rosewater. Add 250 ml (9 fl oz/1 cup) of water. Pour into ice cube trays and freeze. Place the ice cubes into chilled glasses and fill with freshly squeezed orange juice.

manhattan

60 ml (2 fl oz/¹/₄ cup) blended whisky
30 ml (1 fl oz) sweet vermouth
dash of Angostura bitters
lemon peel, for garnish

Fill a glass with ice, then add the whisky, vermouth and bitters. Stir until the alcohol has chilled, then strain into a chilled cocktail glass. Serve with a twist of lemon peel.

long island iced tea

serves 2

30 ml (1 fl oz) vodka
30 ml (1 fl oz) gin
30 ml (1 fl oz) white rum
30 ml (1 fl oz) white tequila
30 ml (1 fl oz) Triple Sec
30 ml (1 fl oz) lemon juice
8 ice cubes
cola, to serve
lemon wedges, to garnish

Place the vodka, gin, rum, tequila, Triple Sec and lemon juice in a cocktail shaker with the ice and shake well. Pour into chilled glasses with ice, and add enough cola to colour the drink. Garnish with the lemon wedges.

peach tree

serves 1

ice cubes, to fill tumbler
60 ml (2 fl oz/1/4 cup) peach syrup
60 ml (2 fl oz/1/4 cup) dark
  Jamaican rum
lime wedge, to garnish

Fill a small tumbler with ice and pour over peach syrup and rum. Stir well and garnish with a wedge of lime. The syrup from poached summer fruit makes an ideal base for this drink.

hot toddy

1/2 teaspoon soft brown sugar
1 strip lemon peel
1 clove
1 cinnamon stick
60 ml (2 fl oz/1/4 cup) whisky

Place all the ingredients into a glass and top with boiling water.

mai tai

ice, to fill cocktail shaker
1 tablespoon lime juice
2 tablespoons Grand Marnier
dash of Angostura bitters
60 ml (2 fl oz/1/4 cup) dark
   Jamaican rum
1 teaspoon grenadine syrup
80 ml (21/2 fl oz/1/3 cup) pineapple juice
2 drops almond essence
ice, extra, to serve
pineapple pieces and mint, to garnish

Fill a cocktail shaker with ice. Add all the remaining ingredients except the extra ice and the garnishes, and shake well. Pour over ice and garnish with fresh pineapple pieces and mint.

mandarin ice
with pomegranate

serves 2

200 ml (7 fl oz) freshly squeezed
   mandarin juice
2 tablespoons sugar syrup
crushed ice, to serve
1/2 pomegranate, juiced, strained

Combine mandarin juice and sugar syrup and pour into glasses filled with crushed ice. Top up each drink with pomegranate juice.

hangover cure

serves 1

60 ml (2 fl oz/¼ cup) Fernet-Branca
30 ml (1 fl oz) Vermouth Rosso
1 tablespoon crème de menthe
ice, to serve

Pour the three liqueurs over ice, mix well and serve.

chicken stock veal stock vegetable stock dashi stock lamb marinade chicken marinade buttered couscous crêpe mixture roasted tomato pasta sauce harissa vinaigrette mashed potato aoïli tahini sauce croutons tamarind water lime sorbet chocolate tart case shortcrust tart case shortcrust tartlet cases cardamom almond bread orange mascarpone vanilla ice cream chocolate ice cream gingerbread

06   basics

raspberry syrup chicken stock veal stock vegetable stock dashi stock lamb marinade chicken marinade buttered couscous crêpe mixture roasted tomato pasta sauce harissa vinaigrette mashed potato aoïli tahini sauce croutons tamarind water lime

chicken stock

makes about 2 litres (70 fl oz/8 cups)

1 whole fresh chicken
1 onion, sliced
2 celery stalks, sliced
1 leek, roughly chopped
1 bay leaf
a few flat-leaf (Italian) parsley stalks
6 peppercorns

Fill a large heavy-based saucepan with 3 litres (105 fl oz/12 cups) of cold water. Cut a fresh chicken into several large pieces and put into the pan.

Bring just to the boil, then reduce the heat to a simmer. Skim any fat from the surface, then add the onion, celery stalks, leek, bay leaf, parsley stalks and peppercorns. Maintain the heat at a low simmer for 2 hours.

Strain the stock into a bowl and allow to cool. Using a large spoon, remove any fat that has risen to the surface.

If a more concentrated flavour is required, return the stock to a saucepan and simmer over low heat. If you are not using the stock immediately, cover and refrigerate or freeze it.

veal stock

makes about 2 litres (70 fl oz/8 cups)

1 kg (2 lb 4 oz) veal bones
2 tablespoons olive oil
2 chopped onions
3 garlic cloves
2 leeks, roughly chopped
2 sliced celery stalks
2 large tomatoes, roughly chopped
1 bay leaf
6 black peppercorns

Preheat the oven to 200°C (400°F/ Gas 6). Put the veal bones and olive oil into a large roasting tin, rub the oil over the bones and bake for 30 minutes. Add the onions, garlic, leeks, celery and tomatoes to the tin. Continue baking for about 1 hour, or until the bones are well browned. Transfer the roasted bones and vegetables to a large heavy-based saucepan and cover with plenty of cold water. Bring to the boil over medium heat, then reduce the heat to a simmer. Skim any fat from the surface, then add the bay leaf and black peppercorns. Cook at a low simmer for 4 hours. Strain the stock into a bowl and allow to cool. Using a large spoon, remove any fat on the surface. Return the stock to a saucepan and simmer over low heat to reduce and concentrate the flavour.

vegetable stock

makes about 2 litres (70 fl oz/8 cups)

40 g (1 1/2 oz) unsalted butter
2 garlic cloves, crushed
2 onions, roughly chopped
4 leeks, coarsely chopped
3 carrots, coarsely chopped
3 celery stalks, thickly sliced
1 fennel bulb, coarsely chopped
1 handful flat-leaf (Italian) parsley
2 sprigs of thyme
2 black peppercorns

Put the butter, garlic and onions into a large, heavy-based saucepan. Put the pan over medium heat and stir until the onion is soft and transparent. Add the leeks, carrots, celery stalks, fennel bulb, parsley, thyme and peppercorns. Add 4 litres (140 fl oz/ 16 cups) of water and bring to the boil. Reduce the heat and simmer for 2 hours. Allow to cool. Strain into another saucepan, using the back of a large spoon to press the liquid from the vegetables. Bring the stock to the boil, then reduce the heat to a rolling boil until the stock is reduced by half.

dashi stock

makes about 2 litres (70 fl oz/8 cups)

30 g (1 oz) dried kombu
20 g (3/4 oz) bonito flakes

Put 2 litres (70 fl oz/8 cups) of cold water and the kombu in a saucepan and slowly bring it to the boil over medium heat. Regulate the heat so that the water takes about 10 minutes to come to the boil. As it nears boiling point, test the thickest part of the kombu; if it is soft to the touch and your thumbnail easily cuts into the surface, remove the kombu.

Let the water come back to the boil, then add half a glass cold water and pour in the bonito flakes. As soon as the stock returns to the boil, remove it from the heat and skim the surface. When the bonito flakes have sunk to the bottom of the pan, strain the stock through a square of muslin or a very fine sieve.

The finished stock should be clear and free of bonito flakes.

Note – Instant dashi is available in most large supermarkets, health food stores or specialty Asian shops.

lamb marinade

125 ml (4 fl oz/1/2 cup) white wine
4 tablespoons olive oil
juice of 1 lemon
1 tablespoon fresh oregano leaves
1 garlic clove, finely chopped

Put the white wine, olive oil, lemon juice, oregano and garlic into a bowl. Add lamb cutlets, fillets or a boned leg of lamb to the marinade. Toss to thoroughly coat the pieces in the mixture. Marinate in the refrigerator for 2–3 hours.

Cook the lamb until it is still a little pink in the centre. Season. Allow to rest for 5 minutes before serving.

chicken marinade

3 tablespoons lemon juice
3 tablespoons olive oil
1 tablespoon dijon mustard
1 teaspoon finely chopped garlic
1 teaspoon thyme
1/2 teaspoon ground white pepper

Put the lemon juice, olive oil, dijon mustard, garlic, thyme and pepper in a large bowl. Add the chicken pieces and toss to coat the pieces in the mixture, then marinate in the refrigerator for 2–3 hours.

Remove the chicken pieces from the marinade and barbecue or roast them until cooked. Season with sea salt and serve.

buttered couscous   serves 4

200 g (7 oz/1 cup) instant couscous
40 g (1¹/2 oz) butter

Bring 250 ml (9 fl oz/1 cup) of water to the boil in a saucepan and throw in the couscous. Take the pan off the heat, add the butter in small pieces and leave it to stand for 10 minutes. Fluff up the couscous with a fork and season well with salt and freshly ground black pepper.

crepe mixture

makes about 10

**125 g (4¹/₂ oz/1 cup) plain
  (all-purpose) flour**
4 eggs
1 teaspoon baking powder
50 g (1³/₄ oz) butter, melted
300 ml (10¹/₂ fl oz) milk

Whisk together the flour, eggs, baking powder, butter and a pinch of salt. Slowly add the milk and whisk until smooth. Allow the batter to sit for a few hours, or preferably overnight.

roasted tomato pasta sauce

serves 4

6 roma (plum) tomatoes
10 basil leaves
1 teaspoon sugar
1 garlic clove
2 tablespoons extra virgin olive oil
1 teaspoon balsamic vinegar

Preheat the oven to 200°C (400°F/ Gas 6). Put the tomatoes on a baking tray and roast in the oven until the skins begin to blacken all over.

Put the tomatoes in a food processor or blender with the basil leaves, sugar, garlic, olive oil and vinegar. Blend to form a thick sauce, thinning the mixture with a little warm water if necessary. This will keep for 2–3 days in the fridge.

harissa

2 red capsicums (peppers)
3 red chillies
2 garlic cloves
1 tablespoon cumin seeds, roasted
  and ground
1 tablespoon coriander seeds, roasted
  and ground
1 large handful coriander (cilantro)
  leaves
1 tablespoon pomegranate molasses
1 teaspoon sea salt
2¹/₂ tablespoons olive oil

Preheat the oven to 210°C (415°F/ Gas 6–7). Put the capsicums in a baking tray and bake until the skin is blistered and blackened. Remove and set aside to cool. Remove the skin and seeds from the capsicums and put the flesh in a food processor with the chillies, garlic, ground spices, coriander, pomegranate molasses and sea salt. Blend to a purée then add the olive oil and process again.

vinaigrette

makes 165 ml (5^1/$_4$ fl oz)

2 tablespoons vinegar
125 ml (4 fl oz/^{1}/$_2$ cup) olive oil
1 teaspoon dijon mustard

Whisk all the ingredients together and season to taste. You may like to add other flavours, such as fresh thyme, basil or rosemary. The vinegar can be replaced with lemon juice.

mashed potato

4 large floury potatoes, peeled
2 tablespoons milk
40 g (1½ oz) butter

Cut the potatoes into pieces. Cook in a saucepan of simmering water for 15 minutes, or until soft. Drain well, then return the potatoes to the saucepan with the milk and butter and mash until smooth. Season with salt and freshly ground black pepper.

aïoli

2 egg yolks
2 large garlic cloves, crushed
300 ml (10¹/₂ fl oz) olive oil
1 lemon, juiced
¹/₄ teaspoon ground white pepper

Whisk together the egg yolks and garlic with a little sea salt. Begin to add the olive oil in a thin stream, whisking continuously. Add a little of the lemon juice and then continue with the remaining oil. Fold in the remaining lemon juice and season to taste with the white pepper and a little sea salt.

tahini sauce

135 g (4³/₄ oz/¹/₂ cup) tahini
1 lemon, juiced
2 tablespoons plain yoghurt
1 teaspoon ground cumin

Put the tahini into a bowl and add the lemon juice, yoghurt, cumin and 3 tablespoons of water. Stir to combine. Serve as a dressing for fish, chicken or with spiced salads.

croutons

makes about 64

6 thick slices of white bread
125 ml (4 fl oz/1/2 cup) oil

Remove the crusts from the bread and cut it into small cubes. Heat the oil in a frying pan and when the surface of the oil starts to shimmer, add the cubes of bread and reduce the heat. Toss the bread in the oil until the croutons are golden brown.

Remove the croutons with a slotted spoon and drain them on paper towels. Season with sea salt and freshly ground black pepper.

tamarind water

500 ml (17 fl oz/2 cups)

100 g (3¹/₂ oz) tamarind pulp

To make tamarind water, put the tamarind pulp in a bowl and cover it with 500 ml (17 fl oz/2 cups) of boiling water. Allow it to steep for 1 hour, stirring occasionally to break up the fibres, then strain.

lime sorbet

serves 4

250 g (9 oz/1 cup) sugar
4–5 limes, zested and juiced

Dissolve the sugar in 1 litre (35 fl oz/4 cups) of water in a saucepan over low heat. Boil for 2–3 minutes, then remove from the heat. Allow to cool. Add the lime juice to the sugar syrup with the zest of 1 lime. Taste, then add a little more lime zest if necessary. Allow to cool. Put in an ice cream machine and churn according to the manufacturer's instructions.

chocolate tart case

makes 1 tart case

160 g (5¹/2 oz) unsalted butter
185 g (1¹/2 cups) plain (all-purpose) flour
2 tablespoons unsweetened cocoa powder

Put all the ingredients in a food processor and whiz to form a paste. If the pastry doesn't ball together, add a dash of chilled water. Cover the pastry in plastic wrap and refrigerate for 30 minutes.

Roll the pastry out as thinly as possible – the easiest way to do this is between two layers of plastic wrap. Line a 25 cm (10 in) tart tin with the pastry. Chill until it is ready to use.

Preheat the oven to 180°C (350°F/ Gas 4). Cover the pastry with a layer of baking paper weighted down with baking weights or uncooked rice. Bake for 15 minutes.

Remove the paper and weights and bake for a further 5 minutes, or until the base of the pastry is cooked through and looks dry.

shortcrust tart case

200 g (7 oz/1²/₃ cups) plain (all-purpose)
  flour
100 g (3¹/₂ oz) unsalted butter
1 tablespoon caster (superfine) sugar

Put the flour, butter, sugar and a pinch of salt into a food processor and process for 1 minute. Add 2 tablespoons of chilled water and pulse until the mixture comes together. Wrap the dough in plastic wrap and chill for 30 minutes.

Roll the pastry out as thinly as possible – the easiest way to do this is between two layers of plastic wrap. Line a greased 25 cm (10 in) tart tin. Chill for a further 30 minutes. Prick the base, line it with crumpled baking paper and fill with baking weights or uncooked rice. Bake in a preheated 180°C (350°F/Gas 4) oven for 10–15 minutes or until the pastry looks cooked and dry. Remove and allow to cool.

Note – Tart cases that are not used immediately can be stored in the freezer for several weeks. Put the tart case in a preheated oven direct from the freezer (there is no need to thaw the case first).

shortcrust tartlet cases

makes 36 tartlet cases

200 g (7 oz) plain (all-purpose) flour
100 g (3½ oz) butter

Put the flour, butter and a pinch of salt into a food processor and process for 1 minute. Add 2 tablespoons of iced water and pulse until the mixture comes together. Wrap in plastic wrap and chill for 30 minutes. Roll the pastry out and cut into rounds. Put into greased patty cake or tartlet tins and chill for a further 30 minutes. Prick the bases, line with crumpled baking paper and fill with baking weights or uncooked rice before placing in a preheated 180°C (350°F/Gas 4) oven for 7–10 minutes. Remove and allow to cool. For a sweet pastry, add 1 tablespoon of caster (superfine) sugar or 1 teaspoon of vanilla extract to the flour and butter mixture.

Note – Tart shells that are not used immediately can be stored in the freezer for several weeks. Place in a preheated oven direct from the freezer (it is not necessary to thaw the tart shells first).

cardamom almond bread

serves 4

3 egg whites

80 g (2³/₄ oz/¹/₃ cup) caster (superfine) sugar

85 g (3 oz/²/₃ cup) plain (all-purpose) flour

2 oranges, zested

90 g (3¹/₄ oz/¹/₂ cup) blanched almonds

¹/₄ teaspoon ground cardamom

Preheat the oven to 180°C (350°F/ Gas 4). To make the almond bread, oil an 8 x 22 cm (3 x 9 in) loaf (bar) tin and line it with baking paper. Whip the egg whites until they are stiff and then slowly whisk in the sugar. When the sugar has been fully incorporated and the whites are glossy, fold in the flour, orange zest, almonds and cardamom. Spoon the mixture into the prepared tin and bake it for 40 minutes.

Cool the almond bread on a wire rack. When it is cold, cut it into thin slices with a serrated knife and spread the slices out on a baking tray. Bake at 140°C (275°F/ Gas 1) for 15 minutes or until the slices are crisp. Allow them to cool on a wire rack before storing them in an airtight container.

orange mascarpone

2 eggs, separated
2 tablespoons sugar
1 tablespoon grated orange rind
250 g (9 oz) mascarpone cheese
1 tablespoon Grand Marnier

Beat the egg whites until they are stiff. Set aside. Beat the egg yolks with the sugar and grated orange rind and, when light and creamy, gently whisk in the mascarpone and Grand Marnier. Fold the egg whites through the mascarpone and chill for 1 hour.

vanilla ice cream

serves 4

8 egg yolks
200 g (7 oz) caster (superfine) sugar
375 ml (13 fl oz/1½ cups) milk
375 ml (13 fl oz/1½ cups) cream
1 vanilla bean, split

Whisk together the egg yolks and sugar until thick and creamy. Put the milk and cream in a saucepan with the split vanilla bean. Bring just to the boil, then pour the hot milk mixture into the sugar and egg mixture while still whisking.

Pour the custard back into the saucepan and continue to stir over a low heat until the custard is thick enough to coat the back of a wooden spoon. Remove the vanilla bean and scrape the seeds into the mixture.

Put the cooled mixture into an ice cream maker and churn according to the manufacturer's instructions.

Alternatively, put it in a freezer-proof container and freeze. Take the ice cream mixture out of the freezer every couple of hours and beat it. This will break up any ice crystals as they form and make the ice cream creamier.

chocolate ice cream

serves 4

375 ml (13 fl oz/1½ cups) milk
250 ml (9 fl oz/1 cup) cream (whipping)
100 g (3½ oz) dark chocolate, roughly
  chopped
4 egg yolks
80 g (2¾ oz/⅓ cup) caster (superfine)
  sugar
2 tablespoons unsweetened cocoa
  powder

Put the milk, cream and chocolate in a heavy-based saucepan over medium heat. Bring the milk and cream just to simmering point, stirring to help the chocolate to melt. Remove the saucepan from the heat. Put the egg yolks and caster sugar in a mixing bowl and whisk until light and foamy. Add the cocoa powder and whisk again. Whisk in a little of the warm chocolate mixture. Add the remaining liquid and whisk to combine. Return the mixture to the clean saucepan. Cook over medium heat, stirring with a wooden spoon, until the mixture thickens and coats the back of the spoon. Strain into a bowl and allow to cool. Churn in an ice-cream machine according to the manufacturer's instructions.

gingerbread

125 g (4 oz) butter
115 g (4 oz/1/2 cup) sugar
90 g (31/4 oz/1/4 cup) molasses
1 egg
175 g (6 oz) plain (all-purpose) flour
1 teaspoon baking powder
2 teaspoons ground ginger
1/2 teaspoon ground cinnamon
2 tablespoons preserved ginger in
  syrup, grated
3 tablespoons brandy

Preheat the oven to 170°C (325°F/
Gas 3). Line a 23 x 13 x 7 cm (9 x 5 x
3 in) loaf (bar) tin. Beat together the
sugar and butter until light and fluffy.
Beat in the molasses and egg. Work
in the dry ingredients and then fold
through the ginger and brandy. Pour
into the tin and bake for 1 hour 45
minutes, or until a skewer inserted
into the centre of the cake comes out
clean. Serve in thick slices.

raspberry syrup

makes 250 ml (9 fl oz/¹/₂ cup)

110 g (3³/₄ oz/¹/₂ cup) sugar
130 g (4³/₄ oz/1 cup) raspberries

Put the sugar, raspberries and 120 ml (4 fl oz) of water into a saucepan and bring to the boil.
Stir until the sugar has dissolved, then reduce the heat to low. Allow to simmer for 5 minutes, remove from the heat and allow to cool. Blend to a purée in a food processor or blender and then strain the purée through a fine sieve into a jug.

glossary

balsamic vinegar

Balsamic vinegar is a dark, fragrant, sweetish aged vinegar made from grape juice. Bottles of the real thing have 'Aceto Balsamico, Tradizionale de Modena' written on the label'.

basil

The most commonly used basil is the sweet or Genoa variety which is much favoured in Italian cooking. Thai or holy basil is used in Thai and Southeast Asian dishes.

black sesame seeds

Mainly used in Asian cooking, black sesame seeds add colour, crunch and a distinct nuttiness to whatever dish they garnish. They can be found in most Asian grocery stores.

bocconcini

These are small balls of mozzarella, often sold sitting in their own whey. They are available from most delicatessens.

brown miso

Brown miso (hatcho miso) is a fermented paste of soya beans, salt and either rice or barley. It is available from Asian shops and health food stores.

bulghur wheat

Bulgur is the key ingredient in tabouli and pilaff. Steamed and baked to minimise cooking time, you can buy these wheat kernels either whole or cracked into fine, medium or coarse grains.

cajun spice mix

This is an American spice blend, easily found in ready mixed packages from most supermarkets. The predominant flavours are cumin, cayenne pepper, chilli, mustard and mixed herbs.

capers

Capers are the green buds from a Mediterranean shrub, preserved in brine or salt. Salted capers have a firmer texture and are often smaller than those preserved in brine. Rinse before using. Capers are available from good delicatessens.

cardamom

A dried seed pod native to India, cardamom is used whole or ground and can be found in the spice section of most supermarkets.

Chinese black beans

These salted black beans can be found either vacuum-packed or in tins in Asian food stores.

Chinese black vinegar

This rice vinegar is sharper than white rice varieties and is traditionally used in stir-fries, soups and dipping sauces.

Chinese five-spice

This aromatic mix of ground spices is made up from black pepper, star anise, fennel seeds, cassia and cloves.

chipotle chillies

Chipotle chillies are available in tins from delicatessens where they are preserved in a smoky rich sauce or they can be bought as large smoked and dried chillies which need to be reconstituted in warm water prior to use.

coconut cream

Slightly thicker than coconut milk, coconut cream is available in tins.

cream of tartar

This fine white powder is the acidic ingredient in baking powder and is used to stablize egg whites.

crème de framboise

A raspberry liqueur.

crème fraîche

A naturally soured cream which is lighter than sour cream, it is available at gourmet food stores and some large supermarkets.

curry leaves

These are the smallish green aromatic leaves of a tree native to India and Sri Lanka. They are usually either fried and added to the dish or used as a garnish at the end.

daikon

Daikon, or mooli, is a large white radish. It can be grated or used in broths. It's available from large supermarkets or Asian grocery stores.

enoki mushrooms

These pale, delicate mushrooms have a long thin stalk and tiny caps. They are very fragile and need only a minimal cooking time.

feta cheese

Feta is a white cheese made from sheep's milk or goat's milk. It must be kept in the whey or in oil during storage or it will deteriorate quickly. Feta is available from delicatessens and most supermarkets.

fish sauce

This is a highly flavoured, salty liquid made from fermented fish and widely used in South Asian cuisine to give a salty, savoury flavour.

Frangelico

A hazelnut-flavoured Italian liqueur sold in a brown bottle shaped like a monk's robe.

galangal

Galangal is quite perfumed and almost a little like camphor. Its root is quite fibrous and hard, making it difficult to chop. Galangal can be bought fresh or sliced and preserved in brine in bottles from Asian stores.

gelatine leaves

Sheet gelatine is available in leaves of varying sizes. If leaves are unavailable, use gelatine powder instead, making sure it is well dissolved in the warm liquid.

goat's curd
This is a soft, fresh cheese made from goat's milk, which has a mild and creamy flavour.

gruyère cheese
A firm cow's milk cheese with a smooth texture and natural rind. It has a nutty flavour and melts easily, making it perfect for tarts and gratins.

haloumi cheese
Haloumi is a semi-firm sheep's milk cheese. It has a rubbery texture which becomes soft when the cheese is grilled or fried.

horseradish
Horseradish is the root of the mustard family — large and white, it has a knobbly brown skin. It is very pungent and has a spicy, hot flavour.

jalapeno chillies
Small pickled jalapeno chillies are available in jars in the Mexican or gourmet section of specialty stores and large supermarkets.

Japanese eggplant (aubergine)
Much smaller and straighter in shape than the conventional eggplant, the Japanese variety also has softer and sweeter flesh.

lavash bread
A Jewish-style bread that is sold fresh as thin unleavened squares or dried in sheets similar to a crispbread.

makrut leaves
Also known as the kaffir lime, the glossy leaves of this Southeast Asian tree impart a wonderful citrusy aroma. Always try and use fresh, rather than dried leaves.

marsala
Perhaps Italy's most famous fortified wine, marsala is available in sweet and dry varieties. Often used in desserts such as zabaglione, it is a superb match with eggs, cream and almonds.

mascarpone cheese
This heavy, Italian-style set cream is used as a base in many sweet and savoury dishes. It is made from cream rather than milk. It is sold in delicatessens and supermarkets.

mirin
Mirin is a rice wine used in Japanese cooking. It is available from Asian grocery stores and most large supermarkets.

miso paste
Miso paste is made of fermented soya beans and other flavourings — wheat, rice or barley. It is used as a flavouring and a condiment.

mustard seeds
Mustard seeds have a sharp, hot flavour that is tempered by cooking. Both brown and yellow are available.

nori

Nori is an edible seaweed sold in paper-thin sheets. Nori sheets are available from most large supermarkets and Asian grocery stores.

palm sugar

Palm sugar (jaggery) is obtained from the sap of various palm trees. If it is very hard it will need to be grated.

pancetta

Pancetta is salted belly of pork. It is sold in good delicatessens and some supermarkets.

papaya

This large tropical fruit can be orange, red or yellow. Sometimes called a pawpaw, they are really part of the custard apple family.

pickled ginger

Japanese pickled ginger is available from most large supermarkets. The thin slivers of young ginger root are pickled in sweet vinegar.

pomegranate molasses

This is a syrup made from the reduction of pomegranate juice. It is available from Middle Eastern specialty stores.

preserved lemon

These are whole lemons preserved in salt or brine, which turns their rind soft and pliable. It is available from delicatessens.

prosciutto

Prosciutto is lightly salted, air-dried ham. It is most commonly bought in paper-thin slices, and is available from delicatessens and large supermarkets.

pumpernickel

A dark, heavy-textured rye bread leavened with a sourdough culture, pumpernickel can be bought from delicatessens and supermarkets.

puy lentils

Originally grown in the volcanic soils of the Puy region in France, these lentils are highly prized for their flavour and the fact that they hold their shape during cooking.

quince paste

Quinces are large, aromatic fruits with a high pectin content. Quince paste can be purchased at most delicatessens.

rice paper wrappers

Rice paper wrappers are made of rice and water paste and come in thin, round or square sheets, which soften when soaked in water. They are available in most large supermarkets or from speciality Asian stores.

rice wine vinegar

Made from fermented rice, this vinegar comes in clear, red and black versions. If no colour is specified in a recipe, use the clear vinegar.

saffron threads

These are the orange-red stigmas from one species of the crocus plant. Saffron should be bought in small quantities and used sparingly.

sambal oelek

A hot paste made from pounded chillies, salt and vinegar, it is available from Asian grocery stores and most large supermarkets.

shiitake mushrooms

These Asian mushrooms have white gills and a brown cap. Meaty in texture, they keep their shape very well when cooked.

shaoxing wine

Shaoxing wine is similar to a fine sherry and is made from glutinous rice. it is available from Asian grocery stores.

sichuan pepper

Made from the dried red berries of the prickly ash tree, which is native to Sichuan in China. The flavour is spicy-hot.

smoked paprika

Paprika is commonly sold as a dried, rich red powder. It comes in many grades from delicate through to sweet and finally hot.

sumac

Sumac is a peppery, sour spice made from dried and ground sumac berries. It is available from most large supermarkets.

tahini

This is a thick paste made from husked and ground white sesame seeds. Tahini is available from health food stores and supermarkets.

tamarind

Tamarind is the sour pulp of an Asian fruit. It is available compressed into cakes or refined as tamarind concentrate in jars.

tofu

This white curd is made from soya beans. Usually sold in blocks, there are several different types of tofu — soft (silken), firm, sheets and deep-fried.

tortillas

This thin, round, unleavened bread is used in Mexican cooking as a wrap. Tortillas are available prepackaged in supermarkets.

turmeric

Turmeric is made from the root of a tropical plant related to ginger.

vanilla

The long slim black vanilla bean has a wonderful caramel aroma. Good quality beans should be soft and not too dry.

white miso

White miso is the fermented paste of soya beans, salt and either rice or barley. It is available from Asian grocery stores.

index

A

aioli 372
apple and blackberry cobbler 242

B

baby eggplant with grilled miso 33
baked figs with pistachios 294
baked leeks with seared salmon 188
baked quinces with orange and cardamom
   almond bread 285
baked salmon with arame and radish salad
   192
banana and berry muffins 230
beef
   beef fillet with horseradish and garlic butter
      200
   braised beef with shiitake mushrooms 104
   chilli beef on witlof leaves 46
   peppered beef with pumpkin mash 215
   seared beef slices with plum sauce and
      mint salad 131
   Vietnamese beef soup 111
beetroot
   beetroot dip 18
   beetroot and goat's cheese salad 120
   roast beetroot salad 69
   saffron mash with roast beets and
      mushrooms 112
   salad of beetroot, chickpeas and feta 136
berry chocolate tart 245
berry granita 282
blackberry fool 278
blood plum and cinnamon jellies 253
braised beef with shiitake mushrooms 104
braised eggplant with water chestnuts 172
brandied oranges with mascarpone 310
burghul salad 66

C

cajun-roasted turkey 163
cardamom almond bread 380
cashew curry 164
cheese
   beetroot and goat's cheese salad 120
   farmhouse cheese with pomegranate and
      radicchio 103
   rocket with baked saffron ricotta 89
   Welsh rarebit 45
chermoula kingfish 171
chicken
   chicken curry 180
   chicken marinade 363
   chicken in a smoked chilli marinade 219
   chicken stock 352
   chipotle chicken 196
   eggplant relish with chicken 128
   grilled chicken with aioli 175
   spiced cumquat chicken 223
chilli
   chicken in a smoked chilli marinade 219
   chilli beef on witlof leaves 46
   chilli mint lamb with saffron vegetables 187
   chilli and vanilla syrup with fresh mango 250
   Mexican spiced chilli beans 144
chipotle chicken 196
chocolate
   bitter chocolate tartlets 274
   chocolate ice cream 384
   chocolate parfait 293
   chocolate tart case 377
cider-glazed pork loin 167
cinnamon French toast 226
cinnamon jam drops 238
cinnamon quince with orange mascarpone
   241

citrus syrup cake 254
coconut and ginger pancakes with five-spice
    duck 93
coconut spiced sweet potato 86
coffee granita 277
couscous, buttered 364
crab tartlets 96
crêpe mixture 365
croutons 374
cumin and lime cookies 261

D
dashi stock 359
dips
    beetroot 18
    eggplant 29
drinks
    berry ice 325
    berry smoothie 317
    chilled knight 321
    classic rusty nail 333
    fig and honey smoothie 314
    greyhound 326
    hangover cure 349
    hot toddy 342
    Long Island iced tea 338
    mai tai 345
    mandarin ice with pomegranate 346
    Manhattan 337
    negroni 329
    peach tree 341
    Pimm's with ginger syrup 322
    rhubarb smoothie 318
    smooth Sambucca 330
duck
    coconut and ginger pancakes with
        five-spice duck 93

ginger duck and udon noodle broth 119
honeyed duck breast with Chinese
    cabbage 168
quince and red wine duck 184
spiced duck breast 211
tamarind duck salad 123

E
eggplant 13
    baby eggplant with grilled miso 33
    braised eggplant with water chestnuts 172
    eggplant dip 29
    eggplant pinwheels 25
    eggplant relish with chicken 128
    eggplant rounds with sweet harissa and
        mint 38
    eggplant and tofu salad 100
    Sichuan eggplant 140
    steamed eggplant salad 85
    sweet potato crisps with baba ghanoush
        58
eggy crêpe roll-up 82

F
farmhouse cheese with pomegranate and
    radicchio 103
fattoush 77
fennel salad 65
figs 9
    baked, with pistachios 294
    honey-spiced 302
fish
    chermoula kingfish 171
    fish with a creamy saffron sauce 208
    fish and saffron broth 132
    fish tagine 159
    lime and cashew blue-eye cod rolls 49

lime and coconut fish 204
seared snapper with spiced butter 155
skewered swordfish with a spiced tahini
     sauce 135
snapper fillets with a pink peppercorn
     dressing 216
spice-crusted fish 199
spiced fish fillets 160
spiced ocean trout 212
summer spiced trout 179
see also seafood
frozen raspberry whip with strawberries 266

G
ginger
     coconut and ginger pancakes with
          five-spice duck 93
     ginger duck and udon noodle broth 119
     ginger hearts 281
     ginger spiced pork cutlets 203
     gingerbread 385
     seared lamb on ginger lentils 183
gravlax with dill dressing on pumpernickel
     50

H
harissa 368
hazelnut meringue with berries 237
honey-spiced figs 302
honeyed duck breast with Chinese cabbage
     168
hummus 41

I
ice cream
     chocolate 384
     ice cream trifles with Turkish delight 258

tamarind ginger ice cream with red papaya
     257
     vanilla 382
J
jaffa mousse 262
jellies
     blood plum and cinnamon 253
     rhubarb 273

L
lamb
     chilli mint lamb with saffron vegetables 187
     lamb fillet with cumin and tomato 156
     lamb marinade 360
     Moroccan lamb 195
     seared lamb on ginger lentils 183
     spiced lentils with lamb cutlets 207
leeks, baked, with seared salmon 188
lentils
     lentil and fennel sausage salad 147
     puy lentil and spinach salad 74
     red lentil soup 115
     rice with vermicelli, parsley and puy lentils
          81
     seared lamb on ginger lentils 183
     spiced lentils with lamb cutlets 207
lime and cashew blue-eye cod rolls 49
lime and coconut fish 204
lime sorbet 376

M
mango, chilli and vanilla syrup with fresh
          mango 250
marinades
     chicken 363
     lamb 360
marinated raspberries with coconut ice 298

meringue
    hazelnut meringue with berries 237
    pine nut meringues with marinated
       raspberries 306
Mexican spiced chilli beans 144
Middle-Eastern summer fruit compote with
    honeyed yoghurt 309
Moroccan lamb 195
muffins, banana and berry 230

N
nectarine salad 290
nuts
    cashew curry 164
    spiced nut blend 30
    spicy nut biscuits 37

O
ocean trout, spiced 212
orange mascarpone 381
oranges
    brandied, with mascarpone 310
    orange juice with rosewater ice cubes
    334

P
pancakes, coconut and ginger, with
    five-spice duck 93
papaya and coconut sambal 70
pasta sauce, roasted tomato 366
pastry
    shortcrust tart case 378
    shortcrust tartlet cases 379
peach and blueberry shortcake 246
peach waffles 233
pears baked in marsala 305
peppered beef with pumpkin mash 215

pine nut meringues with marinated raspberries
    306
pork
    cider-glazed pork loin 167
    ginger spiced pork cutlets 203
    Mexican spiced chilli beans 144
    spiced pork with warm greens 191
    velvet pork belly with wild mushrooms 220
potatoes
    fish tagine 159
    mashed 371
    potato, capsicum and zucchini curry 152
    spiced potato crisps 34
    spiced potatoes 78
prawns, spiced tomato and prawns 176
puy lentil and spinach salad 74

Q
quail eggs with zaatar mix 26
quinces
    baked quinces with orange and cardamom
      almond bread 285
    cinnamon quince with orange mascarpone
    241
    quince and red wine duck 184
    quince and rosewater tarts 297

R
raspberry syrup 387
red lentil soup 115
rhubarb 10
    fool 249
    jelly 273
    syllabub 269
rice with tomatoes and spinach 90
rice with vermicelli, parsley and puy lentils 81
roast beetroot salad 69

roast pumpkin and quinoa salad 143
roast vegetables with rouille 61
roasted tomato pasta sauce 366
rocket with baked saffron ricotta 89
rose-tinged rice pudding 289
rosewater fruit salad 229

S
saffron 14
    fish and saffron broth 132
    saffron mash with roast beets and mushrooms 112
    saffron squid and chive salad 127
salads
    beetroot, chickpeas and feta 136
    beetroot and goat's cheese 120
    burghul 66
    eggplant and tofu 100
    fattoush 77
    fennel 65
    lentil and fennel sausage 147
    nectarine 290
    puy lentil and spinach 74
    roast beetroot 69
    roast pumpkin and quinoa 143
    saffron squid and chive 127
    squid salad with red capsicum and curry vinaigrette 107
    steamed eggplant 85
    tabouleh 22
    tamarind duck 123
    warm banana chilli 73
salt and pepper tofu 53
sausages, lentil and fennel sausage salad 147
seafood
    baked leeks with seared salmon 188

baked salmon with arame and radish salad 192
crab tartlets 96
gravlax with dill dressing on pumpernickel 50
saffron squid and chive salad 127
spiced tomato and prawns 176
squid salad with red capsicum and curry vinaigrette 107
thyme and sumac-seared tuna with minted potatoes 148
see also fish
seared beef slices with plum sauce and mint salad 131
seared lamb on ginger lentils 183
seared snapper with spiced butter 155
shortcrust tart case 378
shortcrust tartlet cases 379
Sichuan eggplant 140
soup
    fish and saffron broth 132
    ginger duck and udon noodle broth 119
    red lentil 115
    spiced carrot 139
    tomato and tofu broth 99
    Vietnamese beef 111
spice-crusted fish 199
spiced fish fillets 160
spiced carrot soup 139
spiced cumquat chicken 223
spiced duck breast 211
spiced lentils with lamb cutlets 207
spiced nut blend 30
spiced ocean trout 212
spiced pan bread 57
spiced pork with warm greens 191
spiced potato crisps 34
spiced potatoes 78

spiced red cabbage 62
spiced tomato and prawns 176
spiced treacle tarts 265
spiced yoghurt with fresh fruit 270
spicy nut biscuits 37
spicy vegetables with couscous 124
squid salad with red capsicum and curry
    vinaigrette 107
sticky black rice 234
sticky date pudding 286
stock
    chicken 352
    dashi 359
    veal 355
    vegetable 356
sweet potato
    coconut spiced sweet potato 86
    sweet potato crisps with baba ghanoush
    58
swordfish, skewered, with a spiced tahini
    sauce 135

T
tabouleh 22
tahini sauce 373
tamarind duck salad 123
tamarind ginger ice cream with red papaya
    257
tamarind water 375
taramasalata 54
tarts
    bitter chocolate tartlets 274
    chocolate tart case 377
    crab tartlets 96
    quince and rosewater tarts 297
    shortcrust tart case 378
    shortcrust tartlet cases 379

spiced treacle tarts 265
thyme and sumac-seared tuna with minted
    potatoes 148
tofu with a black bean sauce 108
tomatoes
    fish tagine 159
    rice with tomatoes and spinach 90
    roasted tomato pasta sauce 366
    spiced tomato and prawns 176
    tomato and tofu broth 99
turkey, cajun-roasted 163

V
vanilla ice cream 382
veal stock 355
vegetables
    roast vegetables with rouille 61
    spiced red cabbage 62
    spicy vegetables with couscous 124
    vegetable stock 356
velvet pork belly with wild mushrooms 220
Vietnamese beef soup 111
vinaigrette 369

W
warm banana chilli salad 73
watermelon squares 42
Welsh rarebit 45
wild rice kedgeree 116
winter fruit crumble 301

Y
yoghurt, spiced, with fresh fruit 270